PRACTICE TESTS

Regina Swopes
Northeastern Illinois University

GOVERNMENT BY THE PEOPLE

BASIC EDITION

22ND EDITION

David B. Magleby
Brigham Young University

David M. O'Brien
University of Virginia

Paul C. Light
New York University

J.W. Peltason
University of California

Thomas E. Cronin
Colorado College

PEARSON
Prentice
Hall

Upper Saddle River, New Jersey 07458

© 2008 by PEARSON EDUCATION, INC.
Upper Saddle River, New Jersey 07458

10 9 8 7 6 5 4 3 2 1

ISBN 10: 0-13-223531-5
ISBN 13: 978-0-13-223531-0

Printed in the United States of America

Contents

Chapter 1
Constitutional Democracy

PART I — LEARNING OBJECTIVES

1.1 What is a democracy?

1.2 How does a democracy differ from other forms of government in practical and theoretical terms?

1.3 What are the defining characteristics of a constitutional government?

1.4 How did the history of American politics before 1787 shape the nature of the Constitution?

1.5 What were the major areas of agreement and disagreement at the Constitutional Convention of 1787?

1.6 What were the most important compromises achieved by the delegates to the Constitutional Convention of 1787?

1.7 What were the most important arguments for and against the ratification of the Constitution?

PART II — PRETEST

1. The idea that a just government must derive its powers from the consent of the people it governs is
   - a. popular consent.
   - b. consent of freedom.
   - c. liberty.
   - d. equality.

2. Which nation's leader was steadfast in his support of President Bush entering into the war in Iraq?
   - a. Great Britain's
   - b. Germany's
   - c. North Korea's
   - d. France's

3. Advocates of democracy argue that the public interest is best discovered by
   - a. consulting top social scientists.
   - b. permitting all adults to have a vote.
   - c. entrusting decision making to political party leaders.
   - d. the creation of philosopher-kings.

4. Democracy as a theory of government is centered on
   - a. the individual.
   - b. political parties.
   - c. interest groups.
   - d. an independent judiciary.

5. Constitutionalism as a part of democratic government serves to
   a. define and limit the government's power.
   b. expand the authority of officials.
   c. protect the rights of the majority.
   d. safeguard against revolution.

6. Which of the following was *not* a weakness of the Articles of Confederation?
   a. Congress had no direct authority over citizens.
   b. Congress could not forbid the states from issuing their own currency.
   c. Congress had to handle all administrative duties (no executive branch).
   d. Congress could only regulate trade between the states, not other nations.

7. A candidate who receives 55 percent of the popular vote has obtained a
   a. majority.
   b. plurality.
   c. consensus.
   d. both choices a and b are correct.

8. The American Revolution began during the
   a. 1750s.
   b. 1760s.
   c. 1770s.
   d. 1780s.

9. The best characterization of the framers of the Constitution would be
   a. visionary idealists.
   b. political philosophers.
   c. experienced, practical politicians.
   d. spokesmen for the average person.

10. The Three-fifths Compromise did not deal with
    a. counting slaves.
    b. taxation.
    c. representation.
    d. treaty ratification.

11. Which of the following is true of young Americans?
    a. They must register to vote before they reach the age of 21.
    b. They vote overwhelmingly Republican.
    c. Lawmakers ignore their concerns.
    d. They are required by law to serve as poll judges.

12. The Puritans of Massachusetts
    a. established a monarchy.
    b. established a theocracy.
    c. established federalism.
    d. permitted their slaves to vote.

13. Taxation without representation began
    a. in Texas.
    b. in 1542.
    c. in Boston.
    d. with the Revolutionary War.

14. What percentage of lawmakers at the federal level are women?
    a. 30
    b. 15
    c. 50
    d. 12

15. Turkey's government is
    a. Islamic.
    b. Christian.
    c. Secular.
    d. a blend of Buddhism and Islam.

PART III — PROGRAMMED REVIEW

Knowledge Objective: To review the many meanings of democracy
1. In a democracy, government derives its authority from its _____.
2. Ancient Greek city-states had a _____ democracy which often turned to mob rule.
3. Most politicians are _____ (honorable, dishonorable) men and women.
4. The word _____ is not used in the Declaration of Independence or in the Constitution.
5. Framers of the Constitution favored the use of _____ rather than democracy.
6. Democracy can be viewed as a system of _____ political structures.
7. _____ is the term used to describe government by the many.
8. A representative democracy is commonly called a _____.
9. A constitutional government normally _____ the power of officials.
10. The central measure of value in a democracy is the _____.
11. The doctrine of _____ makes the community or state the measure of value.
12. _____ or _____ are terms used to describe the right of an individual to set his own goals.
13. In modern America the two major values that are in a state of tension and interaction are _____ and _____.
14. The basic democratic principle involved in elections is one person, _____ vote.
15. In democracies, elections are decided by _____ vote.
16. More important to President Bush than his popularity abroad was securing his _____ in 2004.

Knowledge Objective: To examine conditions necessary for democracy to survive
17. Democracies are most likely to survive when there are positive _____, _____, and _____ conditions.

Knowledge Objective: To explore America's constitutional roots
18. The Founding Fathers insisted that the rights they had as English subjects be spelled out in _____ form.
19. In most American colonies _____ freedom had not been guaranteed.

20. Our Declaration of Independence asserted that the basic rights of all men included _____, _____ and _____.
21. During the period 1781-1789, Americans were governed under their first constitution, the _____.
22. Under the Articles of Confederation, a _____ was created rather than a national government.
23. The need to strengthen the machinery of government was demonstrated during the winter of 1786-1987 by a debtor's protest known as _____.

Knowledge Objective: To discover how the Constitutional Convention of 1787 went about creating a "more perfect union"
24. The framers of the Constitution were guided chiefly by _____ rather than theory.
25. At the Constitutional Convention of 1787, _____ presided; _____ was the highly respected elder statesman.
26. To encourage open discussion and compromise, proceedings of the Constitutional Convention were _____.
27. To break the deadlock over representation, the Connecticut Compromise provided that one house of Congress be based on _____; the other on _____.

Knowledge Objective: To examine the political strategy that led to adoption of the new Constitution
28. Adoption of the new Constitution required ratification by _____ states.
29. Those who opposed adoption of the Constitution were called _____.
30. Hamilton, Jay, and Madison wrote a series of essays urging adoption of the Constitution that is known collectively as _____.
31. Opposition to the new Constitution was largely concentrated in the _____ region.
32. The strategy of those who favored adoption of the Constitution was _____.
33. The Bill of Rights was demanded by the _____.

PART IV — POST-TEST

1. Which of the following is a potential problem for the unilateral approach in war?
   a. burden of cost
   b. resentment by other nations
   c. blame if it fails
   d. all of the above

2. Believers in democracy do not accept
   a. statism.
   b. equality.
   c. individualism.
   d. liberty.

3. In modern America, two concepts once thought to be opposites that exist in an uneasy relationship are
   a. equality and liberty.
   b. federal and unitary government.
   c. oligarchy and autocracy.
   d. socialism and capitalism.

4. Only one of these revolutionary leaders was present at the Constitutional Convention.
   a. Thomas Jefferson
   b. Sam Adams
   c. Patrick Henry
   d. Alexander Hamilton

5. The incident that did most to destroy faith in government under the Articles of Confederation was
   a. the Whiskey Rebellion.
   b. Shays's Rebellion.
   c. the Loyalist revolt.
   d. the Indian uprising.

6. The Founding Fathers favored *all but one* of the following ideas:
   a. a unicameral legislature
   b. a strong executive
   c. an independent judiciary
   d. a more powerful Congress

7. The Connecticut Compromise found a middle ground on the issue of
   a. representation.
   b. slavery.
   c. the court system.
   d. the electoral college.

8. The authors of *The Federalist* include *all but one* of the following:
   a. Hamilton
   b. Jefferson
   c. Madison
   d. Jay

9. To secure ratification, supporters of the Constitution promised
   a. presidential veto power.
   b. a Bill of Rights.
   c. a federal income tax.
   d. a Homestead Act.

10. Only one of the following statements is true of the ratification process.
    a. The opponents tried to get a quick "no" vote.
    b. Most newspapers were Federalist opponents.
    c. Most of the opponents were in rural areas.
    d. Opposition was concentrated in the small states.

11. Who favored extending the right to vote to all white males?
    a. Benjamin Franklin
    b. James Madison
    c. William Penn
    d. Governor Morris

12. Bicameralism refers to
    a. the New Jersey Plan.
    b. the two-party system.
    c. a two-house legislature.
    d. the Confederate Congress.

13. Our present Constitution is an adaptation of the
    a. New Jersey Plan.
    b. Albany Plan.
    c. Virginia Plan.
    d. Connecticut Compromise.

14. The Federalists favored
    a. strong state governments, relative to the central government.
    b. a strong central government, relative to the state governments.
    c. strong ties to Native American tribes.
    d. strong economic ties to Europe.

15. The last state to ratify the Constitution was
    a. New Jersey.
    b. Virginia.
    c. Rhode Island.
    d. Texas.

PART V — TEST ANSWERS

Pretest

1. a
2. a
3. b
4. a
5. a
6. d
7. d
8. d
9. c
10. d
11. c
12. b
13. d
14. b
15. c

Programmed Review

1. citizens
2. direct
3. honorable
4. Democracy
5. republic
6. interdependent
7. Democracy
8. republic
9. limits
10. individual
11. statism
12. Liberty; freedom
13. liberty; equality
14. one
15. majority
16. reelection
17. educational; economic; social
18. written
19. religious
20. life; liberty; pursuit of happiness
21. Articles of Confederation
22. league of friendship
23. Shays's Rebellion
24. experience
25. Washington; Franklin
26. kept secret
27. population; equality
28. nine
29. Antifederalist
30. *The Federalist*
31. back country
32. quick ratification
33. Antifederalists

Post-test

1.	d
2.	a
3.	a
4.	d
5.	b
6.	a
7.	a
8.	b
9.	b

10.	c
11.	a
12.	c
13.	d
14.	b
15.	c

Chapter 2
The Living Constitution

PART I — LEARNING OBJECTIVES

2.1   What are the basic principles of government established by the Constitution?
2.2   What are the three branches of the American Government?
2.3   Why did the framers believe it was so important to create a "separation of powers"?
2.4   What is meant by the term "checks and balances"?
2.5   What is the nature and importance of "judicial review"?
2.6   Why does the meaning of the Constitution evolve over time?

PART II — PRETEST

1. The branch of government most likely to have dominated the framers' opinion was the
    a. bureaucracy.   c. judicial.
    b. executive.   d. legislative.

2. How many states did the ERA lack regarding final ratification?
    a. seven   c. one
    b. four   d. three

3. Law that is higher than human law is dubbed _____ law.
    a. statutory   c. natural
    b. universal   d. constitutional

4. With one exception, ratification of constitutional amendments has been by action of
    a. the president.   c. state conventions.
    b. the Supreme Court.   d. state legislatures.

Match the items in the left column with the correct items from the right column.

5. separation of powers   a. based on custom
6. checks and balances   b. lame duck Congress
7. shared powers   c. allocates power among branches
8. *Marbury v. Madison*   d. independent branches that are
9. impeachment   interdependent
10. informal Constitution   e. established judicial review
                                 f. charges brought by House
                                 g. president signs congressional bill

11. The legislative branch can
    a. pardon persons convicted of federal crimes.
    b. override presidential vetoes.
    c. nominate individuals to serve as federal justices.
    d. go public.

12. Throughout history the federal government has left college education to the
    a. Education Department.
    b. individual and the states.
    c. individual colleges.
    d. Department of the Interior.

13. Which of the following has served to concentrate more power in the executive branch?
    a. poverty
    b. global warming
    c. foreign and economic crises
    d. the Internet

14. To date, how many individuals have been impeached by Congress?
    a. 45
    b. 89
    c. 16
    d. 2

15. Which of the following Supreme Court justices is considered a staunch conservative?
    a. William Brennan
    b. Ruth Bader Ginsburg
    c. Clarence Thomas
    d. David Souter

PART III — PROGRAMMED REVIEW

Knowledge Objective: To analyze the original constitutional arrangements that diffused political power
1. In the United States, the symbol of national loyalty and unity has been the _____.
2. The constitutional arrangement that delegated certain powers to the national government and reserved the rest for the states is called _____.
3. The framers of the Constitution did not fully trust either _____ or the _____.
4. The allocation of constitutional authority among three branches of the national government is known as _____.
5. The framers devised a system of shared power that is described by the term _____.
6. The varying terms of office for national officials were intended to prevent rapid changes by a popular _____.

7. In the United States the ultimate keeper of our constitutional conscience is the
   _____ .

8. The court case that established the practice of judicial review was _____ v. _____.

***Knowledge Objective: To examine the developments that have modified the original
checks and balances system***

9. The president, Congress, and even judges have been drawn together in the
   American system by _____.

10. Originally neither the _____ nor _____ were elected directly by the people.

11. Legislative, executive, and judicial functions are combined in some agencies,
    weakening the concept of _____.

12. In the modern United States, the branch of government that has acquired the
    greatest power is the _____.

13. The British system concentrates power and control in the _____.

Knowledge Objective: To trace evolution of the Constitution by custom and interpretation

14. The customs, traditions, and rules that have evolved over the past two centuries
    are referred to as a(an) _____ Constitution.

15. The structure of the national judicial system was defined by action of _____.

16. _____ realities have increased the importance of the presidency.

17. The Constitution has been adapted to changing times largely through judicial _____.

***Knowledge Objective: To analyze the amendment process and the constitutional
changes made by it***

18. Initiating a constitutional amendment requires a _____ vote by both houses of Congress.

19. Although it has never been used, an amendment can be proposed by a _____ fraction.

20. A proposed amendment must be ratified in three-fourths of the states by either
    their _____ or _____.

21. Congress (has, has not) _____ proposed a great number of amendments.

***Knowledge Objective: To examine politics of the amendment process in cases of ERA
and the D.C. Amendments***

22. In the case of _____ Congress altered the normal process by extending the time
    for ratification.

23. Equal Rights Amendment ratification has been blocked chiefly by a group of
    _____ states.

PART IV — POST-TEST

1. The framers of the Constitution depended heavily on which of the following
   assumptions about human behavior?
   a. Ambition will serve to check ambition.
   b. Most people want to do the right thing.
   c. People are normally apathetic.
   d. Human savagery always lurks below the thin veneer of civilization.

2. The Founding Fathers created a system that
    a. encouraged participatory democracy.
    b. favored the popular majority.
    c. restricted decision making by popular majority.
    d. emphasized prompt, decisive government action.

3. The British democratic system differs from the American system in that
    a. the queen reigns but doesn't rule.
    b. Parliament has only one house.
    c. government authority is concentrated in Parliament.
    d. the High Court exercises judicial review.

4. The original checks and balances system has been modified by *all but one* of the following:
    a. the rise of political parties
    b. creation of regulatory agencies
    c. direct election of senators
    d. giving representatives a four-year term

5. As originally drafted, the Constitution was expected to
    a. cover all foreseeable situations.
    b. be a legal code, combining the framework of government and specific laws.
    c. be a general framework of government.
    d. be a philosophical statement of the relationships among individuals,

6. The Constitution of the United States has been altered without formal amendment by all but one of the following methods:
    a. congressional elaboration
    c. custom and usage
    b. presidential practice
    d. interposition by states

7. Compared to many state constitutions, the national constitution is more
    a. recent.
    c. specific.
    b. complicated.
    d. flexible.

8. The major tool of the courts in checking the power of other government branches has been
    a. impeachment.
    c. judicial review.
    b. habeas corpus.
    d. common law.

9. The constitutional arrangement that limits the power of American officials is known as
    a. separation of powers.
    c. sharing of powers.
    b. prohibitions on authority.
    d. implied powers.

10. During the Revolutionary period, legislatures
    a. were curbed by the checks and balances system.
    b. became the dominant branch of government.
    c. suffered from a steady decrease in power.
    d. governed firmly and wisely.

11. When one party controls the legislative branch and another party the executive branch, this is known as
    a. bicameralism.
    b. divided government.
    c. executive action.
    d. an executive agreement.

12. The electoral college
    a. elects the senate.
    b. selects the Supreme Court justices.
    c. elects the president.
    d. determines which Americans are eligible to vote.

13. The Federal Direct Student Loan program
    a. was devised by the electoral college.
    b. was created by Congress.
    c. began during the Great Depression.
    d. has proven to be an absolute failure.

14. The power of the executive branch has been expanded by
    a. the president's war powers.
    b. new technologies.
    c. direct primaries.
    d. executive orders.

15. The European Court of Justice was created by
    a. the United States Supreme Court.
    b. the United Nations.
    c. the European Union.
    d. the British Parliament.

PART V — TEST ANSWERS

Pretest

1. d	6. g	11. b
2. c	7. d	12. b
3. c	8. e	13. c
4. d	9. f	14. c
5. c	10. a	15. c

Programmed Review

1.	Constitution	13.	legislative branch
2.	federalism	14.	informal
3.	public officials; majority	15.	Congress
4.	separation of powers	16.	Global
5.	checks and balances	17.	interpretation
6.	majority	18.	two-thirds
7.	Supreme Court	19.	constitutional convention
8.	*Marbury v. Madison*	20.	legislatures; ratifying conventions
9.	political parties	21.	has not
10.	president; senators	22.	ERA
11.	checks and balances	23.	southern
12.	executive		

Post-test

1.	a	6.	d	11.	b
2.	c	7.	d	12.	c
3.	c	8.	c	13.	b
4.	d	9.	a	14.	b
5.	c	10.	b	15.	c

Chapter 3
American Federalism

PART I — LEARNING OBJECTIVES

3.1 How would you define federalism?

3.2 What are the advantages and disadvantages of a federal system of government?

3.3 How has American federalism changed in the years since the ratification of the Constitution.?

3.4 What is the relationship between contemporary politics and trends in the size and power of the federal government?

3.5 What role do the federal courts play in defining the relationship among federal, state, and local governments?

3.6 What tools does the federal government have for shaping government policies and practices at the sate level?

PART II — PRETEST

1. The best argument for retention of our federal system would be that it
   a. prevents the centralization of power.
   b. provides cheap, efficient government.
   c. simplifies political party organization.
   d. provides both unity and diversity.

2. The national government has *all but one* of the following powers:
   a. implied
   b. inherent
   c. reserved
   d. delegated

3. The state governments have *only one* of the following sets of powers:
   a. delegated and reserved
   b. reserved and concurrent
   c. direct and inherent
   d. expressed and implied

4. The states' rights interpretation of the Constitution conflicts with one of these concepts:
   a. broad construction
   b. reserved powers
   c. treaty among sovereign states
   d. state governments closer to people

5. The power of the national government that has not been a chief source of its expansion is
    a. to coin money.
    b. to declare war.
    c. to regulate interstate commerce.
    d. to levy taxes.

6. Centralists believe which of the following best defines the power of the national government?
    a. all power specifically delegated by the Constitution
    b. delegated powers plus powers implied from the delegated ones
    c. whatever needs to be done to promote the general welfare
    d. dependent on which party is in power

7. In our history, northerners, southerners, business people, and workers have
    a. consistently agreed on the role of the state governments.
    b. held to a single opinion with respect to national powers.
    c. changed sides in the debate over national-state powers.
    d. shown no discernible pattern of opinion at all.

8. Any group that "has the votes" in Washington is almost certain to favor
    a. a strong national government.
    b. states' rights.
    c. a Supreme Court critical of congressional power.
    d. local government as being closer to the people.

9. The great expansion of our grant-in-aid system occurred during
    a. the New Deal.
    b. the 1960s.
    c. World War I.
    d. World War II.

10. A federal grant that gives a state the right to spend money within a broad category is called a
    a. project grant.
    b. block grant.
    c. community action grant.
    d. grant-in-aid.

11. Interstate compacts must be approved by
    a. Congress.
    b. the Supreme Court.
    c. the United Nations.
    d. the Justice Department.

12. The case of *McCulloch v. Maryland* (1803) involved
    a. the right of a state to tax the federal government.
    b. the right of a state to succeed from the Union.
    c. the power of the president to declare war.
    d. the right of an individual to sue a state.

13. The Civil Rights Act of 1964 is an example of
    a. states' rights.
    b. judicial review.
    c. federal preemption.
    d. divided government.

14. Which of the following former presidents was *not* considered centralist?
    a. Ronald Reagan
    b. Theodore Roosevelt
    c. Abraham Lincoln
    d. Franklin Roosevelt

15. According to the text, the last Supreme Court Chief Justice, William H. Rehnquist, is most remembered for
    a. his defense of affirmative action.
    b. his defense of the right to privacy.
    c. his defense of states' rights.
    d. his defense of gay marriage.

PART III — PROGRAMMED REVIEW

Knowledge Objective: To contrast federalism with alternate forms of government and to discover what advantages it offers Americans
1. A _____ government divides power between a central government and constituent governments.
2. The central government of a confederation exercises no power over _____.
3. A _____ government vests all power in the central government.
4. The relationship between American state and city governments is an example of the _____ form of government.
5. A federal government provides for _____ without uniformity.
6. Under our federal system such questions as divorce, gun control, and school dress codes are _____ issues.
7. The American people are most concerned with _____ politics.

Knowledge Objective: To define how the Constitution allots power and the limitations it imposes
8. The three major powers of Congress upon which national expansion is based are _____, _____, and _____.

9. The Constitution delegates to Congress both _____ powers and _____ powers.
10. As an independent nation, the national government has certain _____ powers.
11. The powers shared by the national and state governments are called _____ powers.
12. The Constitution requires that the national government guarantee to every state a _____ form of government.
13. The _____ clause requires states to enforce civil judgments of other states.
14. The process by which a criminal is surrendered by one state to another is called _____.
15. A binding agreement among states that is approved by Congress is known as a(n) _____.

Knowledge Objective: To trace and explain the growth of the national government and the expanding role of the federal courts
16. Sending federal functions back to the states and local government is called the _____ revolution.
17. The _____ interpretation of the Constitution argued that the national government was created by the states.
18. The centralists' interpretation of the Constitution argued that the national government was an agent of the _____ rather than the states.
19. The concept of implied powers for the national government was first established by the Supreme Court in _____.
20. The Chief Justice of the Supreme Court who first set forth the doctrine of national supremacy was _____.
21. The umpire of the federal system that has favored the national government is the _____.
22. The expansion of the national government can be explained in large part by our evolution from an agrarian society to a(n) _____ society.
23. Our urban society has created a demand for programs operated by the _____ government.
24. Today many Americans identify closely with the national government because of their daily exposure to _____.
25. In 1996, fear of the expansion of the _____ moderated the expansion of government spending.
26. The court action giving Congress the right to assume total power over a state issue is called _____.

Knowledge Objective: To differentiate among the various types of federal grant programs and controls
27. _____ grants involve matching federal-state funds for a specific program.
28. Local communities can receive federal funds directly outside any formula distribution under _____ grants.
29. Federal funds distributed according to formula for a broad purpose are called _____ grants.

30. AFDC was ended under the presidency of _____.
31. Federal regulations that bar state-local discrimination in employment are an example of _____.
32. The national government has indirectly regulated automobile speed limits and minimum drinking ages through its financing of _____ construction.
33. Under the Reagan administration, national control of state and local governments (was, was not) _____ diminished significantly.

Knowledge Objective: To consider the relationship that has developed between national and urban government

34. During the 1960s federal grant policy created a financial bond between the national government and _____.
35. In recent years city officials have found state governments to be (more, less) _____ responsive to their problems.
36. Ronald Reagan "presided over a huge growth of big government at the _____ levels."
37. Most Americans have _____ (strong, weak) attachments to the federal system.
38. In recent years the quality of state government has (improved, deteriorated) _____.

PART IV — POST-TEST

1. The decentralist basic premise is that the Constitution is a
    a. statement of principles.
    b. union of people.
    c. treaty among sovereign states.
    d. document inspired by God.

2. The basic centralist premise is that the Constitution is a supreme law established by the
    a. people.
    b. state.
    c. Creator.
    d. Continental Congress.

3. Federalism can be defined in *all but one* of the following ways:
    a. Political experimentation is encouraged
    b. Governed and governors are in closer contact
    c. Allowances are made for differences
    d. A national majority can more easily implement its program

4. The supreme law of the land is composed of all but the following:
    a. the Supreme Court
    b. the U.S. Constitution
    c. U. S. law
    d. U. S. treaties

18

5. John Marshall's decision in *McCulloch v. Maryland* was that
    a. the government did not have the authority to operate a bank.
    b. state tax powers are unlimited within their boundaries.
    c. Scottish naturalized immigrants can sit on the Supreme Court.
    d. the national government has the authority to carry out its powers in a variety of ways.

6. In interstate relations each state must accept without question one of the following:
    a. a demand for extradition
    b. the enforcement of civil judgment
    c. a Nevada divorce
    d. immediate voting rights for the other state's citizens

7. The average citizen of the United States today
    a. follows closely the activities of the state legislature.
    b. regards the citizens of other states as foreigners.
    c. is in close contact with local and state officials.
    d. is best informed about the national political scene.

8. Throughout our history, business had advocated
    a. states' rights.
    b. national supremacy.
    c. deregulation.
    d. a minimum wage.

9. The present mood of the country with respect to federalism is best described as
    a. confused.
    b. pro city hall.
    c. less revenue-sharing.
    d. states' rights.

10. Under its partial preemption regulations the national government has sought to control
    a. surface mining.
    b. air quality standards.
    c. highway speed limits.
    d. occupational safety.

11. Congressional demands placed upon the states are known as
    a. concurrent powers.
    b. federal mandates.
    c. undue burdens.
    d. interposition.

12. Which of the following activities does the national constitution prohibit the states to engage in?
    a. eminent domain
    b. borrowing money
    c. coining money
    d. chartering banks

13. Interstate relations requires all states to
    a. loan money to other states.
    b. allow citizens of other states to purchase property at less than fair market price.
    c. refuse asylum to persons accused of crimes in other states.
    d. join the United Nations.

14. Which of the following countries has an federal system identical to that of the United States?
    a. Germany
    b. Canada
    c. Switzerland
    d. None of the above

15. Which of the following Supreme Court justices was nominated by President Clinton?
    a. Ruth Bader Ginsburg
    b. Clarence Thomas
    c. David Souter
    d. Arthur Kennedy

PART V — TEST ANSWERS

Pretest

1.	d	11.	a
2.	c	12.	a
3.	b	13.	c
4.	a	14.	a
5.	a	15.	c
6.	c		
7.	c		
8.	a		
9.	b		
10.	b		

Programmed Review

1. federal
2. individuals
3. unitary
4. unitary
5. unity
6. state
7. national
8. war; commerce; tax
9. express; implied
10. inherent
11. concurrent
12. republican
13. full faith and credit
14. extradition
15. interstate compact
16. devolution
17. decentralists'
18. people
19. *McCulloch v. Maryland*
20. John Marshall
21. Supreme Court
22. industrial
23. national
24. television
25. national debt
26. preemption
27. Categorical formula
28. project
29. block
30. Clinton
31. direct orders
32. highway
33. was not
34. cities
35. more
36. state
37. strong
38. improved

Post-test

1. c
2. a
3. d
4. a
5. d
6. b
7. d
8. d
9. a
10. b
11. b
12. c
13. c
14. d
15. a

Chapter 4
Political Culture and Ideology

PART I — LEARNING OBJECTIVES

4.1   What is political culture?
4.2   What are the most important characteristics of American political culture?
4.3   What are the most important American political ideologies?
4.4   How do liberals and conservatives tend to view government and its role in American society?

PART II — PRETEST

1. Most Americans share *all but one* of these following values:
   a. religion
   b. free enterprise
   c. Big Business
   d. free press

2. Americans for the most part *do not believe* in
   a. pragmatism.
   b. free speech.
   c. active political participation.
   d. passive government.

3. Americans do believe in
   a. self-help.
   b. government regulation.
   c. socialism.
   d. a class system.

4. Americans believe that this condition is necessary to make the system work.
   a. unemployment
   b. discrimination
   c. education
   d. uniformity of belief

5. According to most Americans we are not a land of
   a. cooperative endeavors.
   b. opportunity.
   c. common sense.
   d. rugged individualism.

6. For the most part Americans are
   a. anti-intellectual.
   b. theorists.
   c. selfish.
   d. careful spenders.

7. Political culture refers to shared
   a. beliefs.
   b. values.
   c. norms.
   d. all of the above

8. The American dream consists of
   a. enthusiasm for capitalism.
   b. competitive markets.
   c. limited government involvement.
   d. all of these.

9. Grover Norquist would best represent the ideology of
   a. liberalism.
   b. socialism.
   c. conservatism.
   d. libertarianism.

10. The New Right represents a group with a(n) _____ base.
    a. rural
    b. economic
    c. mystical
    d. religious

11. The major criticisms of liberals is that they
    a. will destroy individual initiative and thereby economic growth.
    b. are naïve.
    c. are better at diagnosing problems than providing substantial policies and programs.
    d. are misinformed.

12. Most people in the United States support an economic system that is
    a. pure free market capitalism.
    b. semiregulated or a mixed free enterprise system.
    c. highly regulated by the government.
    d. democratic.

13. The most important source for children learning about American political culture is the
    a. peer group.
    b. school.
    c. family.
    d. mass media.

14. Communism is still intact in
    a. the Czech Republic.
    b. Cuba.
    c. Poland.
    d. Albania.

15. Most of the Western European democracies have
    a. been more influenced by socialism than has the United States.
    b. become more socialist over the past ten years.
    c. changed from socialist to democratic since 1990.
    d. been less influenced by socialism than has the United States.

PART III — PROGRAMMED REVIEW

Knowledge Objective: What are the basic features of American culture and ideology?
1. Classical liberalism stresses the importance of the _____.
2. Liberal political philosophers claimed individuals have certain _____ and the state must be limited.
3. The Constitution, like the American Revolution, defines our nation and its _____.
4. The idea that every individual has a right to equal protection and voting power is called _____.
5. Americans are optimistic about _____, but not about our government.
6. Widely shared beliefs and values are called our political _____.
7. Perhaps our most commonly held belief is that of _____.
8. In the American system of values, the role of government is to _____.
9. Americans believe that (more, less) _____ direct political power should be in the hands of the people.
10. In a broad sense America (does, does not) _____ have an official philosophy.

Knowledge Objective: To trace the demand for additional rights in American experience: The American Dream
11. One of the first rights to be won in America was the right to _____.
12. Inequality of _____ was the result of the growth of corporations.
13. The unregulated growth of American capitalism was challenged by the _____.
14. Huge _____ do not fit into our basic democratic theory.
15. Franklin Roosevelt declared that all Americans had the right to adequate _____ care.
16. Roosevelt also said that every American had the right to a useful _____.
17. The gap between rich and poor in the United States has _____ in recent years.
18. Americans dream of acquiring _____.
19. The American Dream includes (inequality, equality) _____ of income.
20. Most Americans today support a semiregulated or _____ free enterprise system.

Knowledge Objective: To distinguish between liberal and conservative public policies
21. Modern _____ political leaders favor greater government activity.
22. _____ leaders believe that national progress is possible.
23. Environmentalism is exemplified by _____ parties in Europe and America.
24. Private property rights and free enterprise are basic beliefs of _____.
25. _____ believe that most people who fail are personally responsible for their failure.
26. A brand of conservatism that is more radical, the New _____ has emerged in recent years.
27. Conservatives are criticized for not endorsing policies against racism and _____.
28. _____ favor an expanded government that would own the means of production and distribution.

29. _____ favor a severely curbed role for government in domestic and foreign affairs.

Knowledge Objective: To define the basic political tension in modern America
30. Our national political life is based on a (carefully defined, vague) _____ theory.
31. American political parties are (more, less) _____ ideological than European parties.
32. Tolerance is most prevalent among _____ (liberals, conservatives).
33. Conservatives show more concern for the rights of _____ while liberals show more concern for the rights of the _____.
34. Conservatives prize the private sector over the _____ sector.
35. Conservatives believe that America has become too _____.

PART IV — POST-TEST

1. Which one of the following groups wants the least government?
   a. Libertarians
   b. Conservatives
   c. Liberals
   d. Socialists

2. Which group demands the most government?
   a. Socialists
   b. Conservatives
   c. Libertarians
   d. Greens

3. Former senator Rudman questions the GOP alliance with which group?
   a. New Right
   b. Environmentalists
   c. Conservatives
   d. Libertarians

4. A major barrier to equality of opportunity today is
   a. failure to vote.
   b. lack of education.
   c. unequal start.
   d. high taxes.

5. When the Great Depression began we had
   a. unemployment compensation.
   b. bank deposit guarantees.
   c. regulation of security exchanges.
   d. the vote for women.

6. The American president most responsible for greatly expanding the rights of all Americans was
   a. Truman.
   b. Eisenhower.
   c. Hoover.
   d. FDR.

7. Those who favor expansion of government control over drinking, drugs, abortion, prayer, and life style are
   a. Conservatives.
   b. New Right.
   c. Liberals.
   d. Libertarians.

8. The most important source of the American political culture is the
   a. school.
   b. family.
   c. mass media.
   d. church or synagogue.

9. The political group who today advocates the withdrawal of our forces from Europe and the decriminalization of drug possession is
   a. Conservatives.
   b. Liberals.
   c. Libertarians.
   d. Socialists.

10. In today's world the greatest conflict is between the free market enterprise system and
    a. socialism.
    b. equality of opportunity.
    c. private property.
    d. voting rights.

11. Which of the following is *not* a shared value of Americans?
    a. domination
    b. liberty
    c. equality
    d. justice

12. Which value is stressed by the Green Party in the United States?
    a. an energy efficient economy
    b. the integrity of natural systems
    c. agriculture which replenishes the soil
    d. all of the above

13. The organizing device for the postindustrial era is
    a. education.
    b. knowledge.
    c. high technology.
    d. skill.

14. A number of political scientists argue that the American party system has been shaped by
    a. labor unions.
    b. great leaders.
    c. world events.
    d. realigning elections.

15. A social division based on national origin, religion, language, and a sense of attachment may form a(n)
    a. ethnicity.
    b. cultural group.
    c. national group.
    d. race.

PART V — TEST ANSWERS

Pretest

1. c	4. c	7. d	10. d	13. c
2. d	5. a	8. d	11. a	14. b
3. a	6. a	9. c	12. b	15. a

Programmed Review

1. individual
2. natural rights
3. values
4. political equality
5. people
6. culture
7. liberty
8. serve the people
9. more
10. does not
11. vote
12. wealth
13. Great Depression
14. corporations
15. medical
16. job
17. grown
18. property
19. inequality
20. mixed
21. liberal
22. Liberal
23. Green
24. conservatives
25. Conservatives
26. Right
27. sexism
28. Socialists
29. Libertarians
30. vague
31. less
32. liberals
33. victims of crime; accused
34. public
35. permissive

Post-test

1. a	4. c	7. b	10. b	13. b
2. a	5. d	8. b	11. a	14. c
3. a	6. d	9. c	12. d	15. a

Chapter 5
The American Political Landscape

PART I — LEARNING OBJECTIVES

5.1   How do Americans define themselves?

5.2   What challenges have been created by the migration of the American middle class to the suburbs?

5.3   What is the relationship between American sectional diversity and American politics?

5.4   What is the relationship between social and economic status, on the one hand, and political attitudes and participation on the other?

PART II — PRETEST

1. The tendency of every person to make sweeping judgments based on their limited personal experience is called
    a. ethnocentricism.   c. experience.
    b. wisdom.   d. selfishness.

2. The most distinct geographical region in the United States is the
    a. Midwest.   c. South.
    b. Southwest.   d. West.

3. Only one of these cities does *not* have a majority black population.
    a. Phoenix   c. Richmond
    b. Baltimore   d. New Orleans

4. Which of the following is *not* a gender issue?
    a. sexual harassment   c. peace
    b. child support   d. English as the official language

5. The most politically underrepresented group has been
    a. Asians.   c. blacks.
    b. Hispanics.   d. women.

6. The most potent politically active group has been
    a. college students.   c. the poor.
    b. the elderly.   d. the common man.

7. A popular theory that explains the unity achieved by Americans is the
   a. salad bowl.
   b. melting pot.
   c. welding.
   d. ethnicity.

8. Compared to most industrialized countries the United States does *not* have a high degree of _____ awareness
   a. social class
   b. religious intolerance
   c. personal achievement
   d. acceptance of a leisure class

9. In recent years the South has given its vote for president to
   a. Republicans.
   b. Democrats.
   c. no decisive pattern.
   d. varied.

10. Black migration from the South occurred chiefly after
   a. 1865.
   b. 1950.
   c. 1970.
   d. 1900.

11. Compared to women in other Western democracies, American women tend to vote
   a. more often.
   b. more compassionately.
   c. across party lines.
   d. less than their Western European counterparts.

12. A characteristic of individuals that predicts their political behavior is called
   a. political predisposition.
   b. political socialization.
   c. reinforcing cleavage.
   d. ethnocentrism.

13. Aside from race, the most important factor in explaining views on issues, partianship, and ideology may be
   a. ethnicity.
   b. religion.
   c. wealth.
   d. income.

14. As the population base of the city shifts from richer to poorer,
   a. service needs in the city increase.
   b. the tax base of the city declines.
   c. there is more crime.
   d. both a and b.

15. All of the following are true *except*
    a. economically, African Americans are much worse off than whites.
    b. one-half of all African Americans are below the poverty line.
    c. the median income for African Americans is around $34,000.
    d. African Americans' net worth is less than that of whites.

PART III — PROGRAMMED REVIEW

Knowledge Objective: To trace the roots of the American people
1. Proposition 187 in California dealt with the issue of _____.
2. The tendency to generalize from our own experience is called _____.
3. The belief that we have a foreordained role to become a world power is called _____.
4. The most distinct section of the United States is the _____.
5. After the Civil War the South normally supported the _____ party.
6. The West has developed a strong sense of _____.
7. Most Americans now live in _____ areas.
8. The migration of white Americans to the suburbs after World War II is known as the _____.
9. Migration of the whites from the cities has resulted in a(n) _____ tax base.

Knowledge Objective: To distinguish the various elements in our diverse society
10. Children normally learn their political values within the _____.
11. When cultural values are in conflict the result is called _____ cleavages.
12. Politically, the United States compared to Ireland has less emphasis on _____.
13. The first Jewish vice presidential candidate for a major party was Senator _____ in 2000.
14. The mass migration of blacks to the city gave them greater _____ power but left them with limited _____ power.
15. Nearly _____ of the blacks fall below the poverty level.
16. According to the text, Hispanics are politically _____.
17. Hispanics can be of any _____.
18. Generally speaking older ethnic groups have greater _____ power than newer ethnic groups.
19. Compared to the women in other countries, American women vote _____ (more, less).
20. The largest segment of Americans are _____.
21. Women for the most part (do, do not) _____ support female candidates.
22. As women age, the earnings gap _____.
23. Significant political difference between men and women is called the _____.
24. A defining characteristic of religion in America is the variety of _____.

25. African Americans traditionally support the _____ party.

26. Widespread income distribution results in political _____.
27. One of the most important means for Americans to achieve economic and social mobility is _____.
28. Originally most Americans worked as _____.
29. Today America is known as a _____ society.
30. In terms of social class most Americans believe that they are _____ class.
31. In recent years the American Dream has been challenged by foreign _____.

PART IV — POST-TEST

1. Democratic strengths in the South have been greatest in elections for
   a. president.
   b. U.S. Senate.
   c. representatives.
   d. no pattern.

2. The state with the largest population is
   a. New York.
   b. Pennsylvania.
   c. California.
   d. Texas.

3. Fundamentalist Christians have an agenda that includes *all but one* of the following:
   a. return of school prayer
   b. outlaw abortion
   c. outlaw guns
   d. restrict homosexuals

4. The population of American cities has *all but one* of the following characteristics:
   a. poor
   b. black
   c. independent
   d. democratic

5. Black unemployment is a result of *all but one* of the following:
   a. limited education
   b. youth
   c. depressed urban areas
   d. limited political power

6. Most Asian Americans live in *all but one* of the following states:
   a. Michigan
   b. Hawaii
   c. Washington
   d. California

7. Recent Asian-American migration has been from *all but one* of the following:
   a. Korea
   b. Japan
   c. Asia
   d. Southeast

8. The fastest growing ethnic group in the United States is
   a. Hispanics.
   b. African Americans.
   c. Asians.
   d. Native Americans.

9. The gray lobby has *all but one* of these political assets:
   a. mostly male
   b. disposable income
   c. discretionary time
   d. focused issues

10. American unity is strengthened by *all but one* of the following:
    a. the American Dream
    b. work ethic
    c. economic opportunity
    d. foreign investment

11. Population growth patterns include all of the following *except*
    a. in the West growth is explained by younger persons.
    b. growth in the South is primarily explained by growth in the population that is over age 65.
    c. Sun Belt states have experienced greater economic growth than most other areas.
    d. there has been a resurgence of industrial growth in the New England states.

12. Something given with the expectation of receiving something in return is called
    a. bundling.
    b. amicus curiae.
    c. quid pro quo.
    d. lobbying.

13. Groups which lobby for a limted goal are called
    a. short-term interest groups.
    b. limited issue groups.
    c. public interest groups.
    d. single issue groups.

14. Which political party received the most support from 501-C organizations in 2004?
    a. Democrat
    b. Republican
    c. Green
    d. Libertian

15. Most interest groups try to
    a. be nonpartisan.
    b. find a "winner" to support.
    c. target a single political party.
    d. target challengers for public office.

PART V — TEST ANSWERS

Pretest

1.	a	6.	b	11.	d
2.	c	7.	b	12.	a
3.	a	8.	a	13.	d
4.	d	9.	a	14.	d
5.	b	10.	b	15.	b

Programmed Review

1. immigration
2. ethnocentricism
3. manifest destiny
4. South
5. Democratic
6. individualism
7. metropolitan
8. white flight
9. declining
10. family
11. cross-cutting
12. religion
13. Lieberman
14. political; economic
15. one-third
16. underrepresented
17. race
18. economic
19. less
20. women
21. do not
22. widens
23. gender gap
24. denominations
25. Democratic
26. stability
27. education
28. farmers
29. postindustrial
30. middle
31. competition

Post-test

1. c	6. a	11. d
2. c	7. b	12. c
3. c	8. a	13. d
4. c	9. a	14. b
5. d	10. d	15. a

Chapter 6
Interest Groups: The Politics of Influence

PART I — LEARNING OBJECTIVES

6.1 What is an interest group?
6.2 How have interest groups changed over the course of American history?
6.3 What is a lobbyist?
6.4 What role does money play in the relationship between interest groups and political decision makers?
6.5 How much influence do interest groups have?
6.6 How do lobbyists shape the political decision-making process?
6.7 What efforts have been made to limit the influence of interest groups on elections and political decision making?

PART II — PRETEST

1. The loyalty of interest group members is often diminished by their
   a. overlapping allegiances.   c. limited time.
   b. inability to pay dues.   d. religious convictions.

2. Nearly all adult Americans belong to a/an _____ interest group.
   a. social   c. ideological
   b. religious   d. occupational

3. In recent years the great expansion of PACs has been in the _____ sector.
   a. labor   c. business
   b. professional   d. farming

4. The chief influence of PACs in election campaigns has been their
   a. contributions.   c. door-bell ringing.
   b. advice.   d. professional aid.

5. In its efforts to control factions and interest groups, the United States has rejected
   a. their prohibition.   c. regulating their activity.
   b. publicizing their activity.   d. lobbying.

6. AIPAC is an interest group that promotes the interest of
   a. the Arab states.   c. senior citizens.
   b. Israel.   d. labor unions.

7. Which one of the following interest groups cuts across religious, ethnic, and economic groups?
    a. American Medical Association   c. Knights of Columbus
    b. American Soybean Association   d. Young Americans for Freedom

d 8. The interest group that has advocated an open political process and electoral reform is
    a. the National Rifle Association.   c. the Trilateral Commission.
    b. Nuclear Freeze.   d. Common Cause.

b 9. Efforts to represent the general welfare are thwarted by _____ groups.
    a. public interest   c. occupational
    b. single cause   d. organized

b 10. In the 2004 general election, the most active new interest group was
    a. the National Rifle Association.   c. the Sierra Club.
    b. America Coming Together.   d. Pro-Choice America.

a 11. AIPAC is an example of a
    a. foreign policy interest group.   c. public interest group.
    b. government interest group.   d. single issue group.

a 12. A large body of people who are interested in a common issue, idea, or concern that is of continuing significance and who are willing to take action on that issue are called
    a. movements.   c. factions.
    b. associations.   d. groups.

a 13. When groups find the political channels closed to them, they may turn to the
    a. courts.
    b. interest groups.
    c. creation of a political party.
    d. United Nations.

b 14. Which of the following is *not* a way the AARP encourages potential members to join their organization?
    a. free subscription to a magazine
    b. oppose prescription drug benefits
    c. speaks out on issues of concern to older citizens
    d. voter education drives

b 15. Networks of mutually supporting relationships among interest groups, congressional committees and governmental agencies that share a policy concern are called
   a. co-opts.
   c. issue organizations.
   b. iron triangles.
   d. wired networking.

PART III — PROGRAMMED REVIEW

Knowledge Objective: To examine factions as a force in politics
1. James Madison's famous essay on the role of factions is called *The Federalist, No. 10*.
2. Madison believed that popular government normally resulted in instability, injustice, and confusion because it encouraged the growth of *factions*.
3. Any group whose members share attitudes and try to achieve certain aims and objectives is called an *interest* group.
4. Movements normally arise when segments of the population find that the dominant political culture does not share their *value*.
5. Movement politics normally are successful in raising the political _____ of their followers. *conscience*
6. The "paycheck protection" initiative was against *labor unions*.
7. Interest groups are also called *special interests*.

Knowledge Objective: To describe the various kinds of interest groups
8. Nearly every employed person belongs to an _____ interest group. *8. Occupational*
9. The major farm interest group is _____; labor's largest group is _____; and the largest business group is _____. *9. American Farm Bureau; AFL-CIO; Chamber of Commerce*
10. Common Cause is an example of a *public interest* group.
11. The highly articulate spokesman for a conglomerate of consumer interest groups and the Green Party's presidential candidate in 2000 was *Ralph Nader*.
12. The ACLU is an example of an _____ interest group. *ideological*
13. _____ groups focus on highly specialized political issues. *Single interest*

Knowledge Objective: To investigate the techniques of interest group politics
14. Central tests of a group's power are its _____ and _____. *Size; involvement*
15. The most cohesive interest groups are those with a _____ power structure. *Centralized*
16. The AARP uses _____ to combat the free-rider problem. *incentives*
17. Civil liberties, environmental, and black groups have used _____ as a weapon to achieve their goals. *litigation*
18. The Federal _____ lists regulations of executive departments/agencies. *Register*
19. The employee of an interest group who presents its point of view to legislators is called a _____. *lobbyist*
20. The employment cycle from government to interest group is known as the _____. *revolving door*
21. Lobbyists have the _____ needed by legislators for policy making. *Specialized knowledge*

22. The newest form of interest groups that back candidates and raise money are
    _____. PACs

23. The great expansion of PACs during the 1980s was among _business_ _____ interest
    groups.

24. Contributors to PACs normally (do, do not) _do not_ _____ demand immediate payoffs if
    their candidate wins.

25. Big labor's political arm is called _____. COPE

26. PACs can _bundle_ their contributions in order to boost their clout with elected
    officials.

27. _____ is not a major criterion used by big corporations in financing the
    campaigns of congressional candidates. Party

28. Most PAC funds go to _____ congressmen. incumbent

PART IV — POST-TEST

1. James Madison urged the control of contending factions under the new constitution
   in an essay called
   - a. Failing Factions.
   - b. Letters of the Federal Farmer.
   - c. Downing #9.
   - d. *The Federalist,* No. 10.

2. Many of the strongest "unions" in terms of their political effectiveness are _____
   organizations.
   - a. recreational
   - b. racial
   - c. feminine
   - d. professional

3. Those organizations that insist that they are solely devoted to the public welfare are
   called
   - a. ideological.
   - b. professional.
   - c. public interest.
   - d. political.

4. One of the following factors is normally *not* critical in determining a group's
   political strength.
   - a. strong leadership
   - b. size of membership
   - c. unity of membership
   - d. geographical distribution

5. Ralph Nader, the American Civil Liberties Union, and the NAACP have depended
   heavily upon _____ to influence public policy.
   - a. litigation
   - b. direct action
   - c. persuasion
   - d. campaign spending

6. The political arm of a business/labor/professional interest group is called a
   - a. LEG.
   - b. GYP.
   - c. CON.
   - d. PAC.

7. The least important factor in determining the support of candidates by business PACs is their
    a. voting record.   c. winability.
    b. incumbency.   d. party affiliation.

8. The Lobbying Disclosure Act of 1995 did *all but one* of the following:
    a. reformed campaign finances
    b. expanded the definition of a lobbyist
    c. increased disclosure requirements
    d. required lawyer-lobbyists for foreign entities to register

9. When a group finds the normal political processes closed, they are apt to turn to
    a. propaganda.   c. litigation.
    b. rule-making.   d. persuasion.

10. Groups free to make unlimited contributions to groups that engage in efforts to elect or defeat candidates through the mail, on the phone, or in person, are called
    a. small PACs.   c. "no-TV" PACs.
    b. 527s.   d. 632s.

11. Which "Founding Father" wrote the most common and durable source of factions has

been the various and unequal distribution of property"?
    a. James Madison
    b. Thomas Jefferson
    c. Benjamin Franklin
    d. Alexander Hamilton

12. The political power of interest groups is directly related to
    a. the size of the group.
    b. cohesiveness.
    c. their close ties to only one political party.
    d. resources.

13. _____ is a term used by the founders of this country to refer to political parties and special interests or interest groups.
    a. Advocacy group   c. Faction
    b. Movement   d. Issue group

14. To members of Congress, the most important thing lobbyists provide is
    a. information.
    b. influence.
    c. analysis.
    d. money.

15. Associations can gain a forum for their views by filing
    a. writs of mandamus.
    b. amicus curiae briefs.
    c. writs of certiorari.
    d. none of the above unless they are parties to the dispute

PART V — TEST ANSWERS

Pretest

1.	a	9.	b
2.	d	10.	b
3.	c	11.	a
4.	a	12.	a
5.	a	13.	a
6.	d	14.	b
7.	d	15.	b
8.	d		

Programmed Review

1. *The Federalist*, No. 10
2. factions
3. interest
4. values
5. conscience
6. labor unions
7. special interests
8. occupational
9. American Farm Bureau; AFL-CIO; U.S. Chamber of Commerce
10. public interest
11. Ralph Nader
12. ideological
13. Single interest
14. size; involvement
15. centralized
16. incentives
17. litigation
18. *Register*

40

19. lobbyist
20. revolving door
21. specialized knowledge
22. PACs
23. business
24. do not
25. COPE
26. bundle
27. Party
28. incumbent

Post-test

1.	d	9.	c
2.	d	10.	b
3.	c	11.	a
4.	b	12.	d
5.	a	13.	d
6.	d	14.	d
7.	d	15.	c
8.	a		

Chapter 7
Political Parties: Essential to Democracy

PART I — LEARNING OBJECTIVES

7.1   Why is it so difficult for a viable third party to emerge in the American political system?
7.2   How are political parties financed?
7.3   What are the most important sources of money for each of the two major political parties?
7.4   What role do political parties play in the election process?
7.5   How are the two largest American political parties organized?
7.6   How have the nature and function of American political parties changed over the course of American history?
7.7   What role do the two major political parties play in American government and politics?

PART II — PRETEST

1. The percentage of party members who vote together on roll call votes is called
   a. patronage.
   b. party unity scores.
   c. proportionality.
   d. dealignment.

2. Managing the presidential campaign is the job of
   a. the national committee.
   b. the national chairman.
   c. the attorney general.
   d. the presidential press secretary.

3. The first Republican party was led by
   a. Jefferson.
   b. Hamilton.
   c. Washington.
   d. Adams.

4. Candidates are selected by their parties because of
   a. party loyalty.
   b. personal appeal.
   c. endorsement by party leaders.
   d. ideological correctness.

5. When voters may choose what ballot they will vote in a primary, it is called
   a. closed.
   b. open.
   c. realignment.
   d. dealignment.

6. The purpose of a political party is
    a. to recruit potential officeholders.
    b. to simplify alternatives.
    c. to unite the electorate.
    d. all of the above.

7. A striking characteristic of third parties is that they
    a. advance controversial issues and ideas.
    b. are always radical.
    c. are always conservative.
    d. have no place in the American system.

8. The most significant factor influencing the character of American political parties is
    a. the federal system.
    b. the national convention.
    c. the party seniority system.
    d. the presidential primary.

9. Which of the following is *not* a present-day function of political parties?
    a. distribution of welfare handouts
    b. stimulation of interest in public affairs
    c. recruitment of political leadership
    d. linkage between the mass public and government

10. A major cause for the persistence of the two-party system in the United States is that
    a. the major parties have become disciplined and issue-oriented.
    b. election districts have a single incumbent.
    c. third parties have failed to point up issues.
    d. major party ideas and platform are too much like religious dogma.

11. Who decides which candidates get party campaign funds for senatorial campaigns?
    a. the national chairman
    b. the chair(s) of the senatorial campaign committees
    c. the party caucus
    d. the national convention chair

12. Although parties play a significant role in elections, the authors contend that their most important role is in
    a. collecting campaign contributions.
    b. preparing for the next election.
    c. serving as a symbol of democracy.
    d. the operation of government.

13. Minor parties in the United States have usually been organized around
    a. race.
    b. ideology.
    c. a candidate.
    d. both b and c

14. Which of the following is *not* true of the 2002 midterm elections?
    a. The president's party gained seats.
    b. Democrats lost every gubernatorial race.
    c. The Republicans picked up seats in both the House and the Senate.
    d. President George W. Bush campaigned aggressively for Republican candidates.

15. Which best describes an economic policy that opposes governmental interference in economic affairs beyond what is necessary to protect life and property?
    a. laissez-faire
    b. supply side
    c. Keynesian
    d. demand side

PART III — PROGRAMMED REVIEW

Knowledge Objective: To analyze what parties do for democracy
1. Parties organize the _____ by choosing candidates to run under their label.
2. Parties failed to unify the electorate in the 1860s over the issue of _____.
3. Politicians are nominated largely on the basis of their qualifications and personal appeal, not _____ loyalty.
4. The outcomes of American elections (do, do not) _____ make a difference in public policy.
5. Party _____ include simplifying issues, stimulating interest, uniting different segments of society, and recruiting political leadership.
6. Political parties formerly served as a kind of employment agency through their control of _____.
7. As a method of choosing candidates, the caucus was replaced by party _____ which on the state level were replaced by the _____.
8. The American two-party system is maintained because in our single election districts only _____ candidate wins.
9. Third parties organize around a _____ or an _____.

Knowledge Objective: To review the long history of American political parties
10. The Federalist party was challenged by the first _____ party, headed by Jefferson.
11. Today's _____ party (Grand Old Party) arose out of the Civil War.
12. _____ created a party coalition of Southerners, labor, farmers, the unemployed, and suburbanites.
13. Until the 1994 midterm elections, Republicans have been more successful in winning _____ elections than congressional elections.

Knowledge Objective: To review the present state of our parties

14. Modern political parties have (more, less) _____ voice in choosing presidential candidates.
15. Both parties today are (moderate, sharply different) _____ in policies and leadership.
16. Political parties in the United States are primarily organized to win political _____.
17. The reason why political parties are so decentralized is the _____ basis of our government.
18. In recent years the party's national committee has given the state and county organizations _____ money.
19. The supreme authority in both political parties is the national _____ convention.
20. A national_____ heads each of the two major parties.
21. Party platforms try to _____ differences in order to appeal to as many voters as possible.
22. In the U.S. Congress, the committee chairs of all the standing committees come from the _____ party.
23. Democrats are (more, less) _____ likely than Republicans to give government a large role in social-economic programs.
24. Today the party remains an important consideration in the naming of _____ judges.
25. A _____ primary is one in which voters are restricted to a single party in the primary election.
26. Party _____ is the single best predictor of the vote.
27. Efforts to reshuffle existing political coalitions is called _____.
28. Pure _____ are the least apt to vote.
29. The main charges against political parties is failure to take meaningful stands on _____ and weak _____.
30. The technology that has had the most impact on elections is the _____.

Knowledge Objective: Discuss "Can parties be saved?"; Campaign Finance, 2002

31. One reform by the GOP was to give _____ more control over presidential races.
32. Democrats created "_____" positions for elected officials/party leaders.
33. Soft money donors may contribute to _____ groups in the future.
34. According to 2002 campaign finance reforms, a deduction up to _____ can go to party committees.

PART IV — POST-TEST

1. The person least likely to vote is a
   a. strong Democrat.
   b. weak Republican.
   c. pure Independent.
   d. middle-of-the-road Democrat.

2. The _____ party evolved out of the crisis over slavery.
   a. Whig
   b. Democratic
   c. modern Republican
   d. Second Federalist

3. Third-party leaders have included all of the following *except*
   a. Ralph Nader.
   b. Ross Perot.
   c. George Wallace.
   d. Governor Jerry Brown.

4. In both major parties, the supreme authority is the
   a. candidate.
   b. party chairman.
   c. national nominating convention.
   d. primaries.

5. The grass roots of each party is
   a. in the deep south.
   b. in the western states.
   c. at the city, town, ward, and precinct level.
   d. at the family, church, and school level.

6. The party that put together a grand coalition lasting from the Civil War until 1932 was
   a. Democratic.
   b. Republican.
   c. Whigs.
   d. Federalist.

7. Under the dealignment theory, people have
   a. become Reagan Democrats.
   b. become presidential Democrats.
   c. abandoned both parties to become Independents.
   d. returned to liberal Democrats.

8. When a voter must be registered in a party to vote in the primary, it is called
   a. closed.
   b. open.
   c. direct.
   d. crossover.

9. Republicans in the past decade have *not* emphasized one of the following reforms:
   a. membership recruitment
   b. racial and sex quotas
   c. grassroots organization
   d. candidate training programs

10. Both major political parties today are
    a. relatively weak.
    b. strong coalitions.
    c. class-oriented.
    d. tightly disciplined.

11. If states organize the ballot in party columns, it makes it somewhat easier for voters to vote
    a. for candidates from different parties.
    b. with a "one punch."
    c. for each candidate by office.
    d. a straight ticket.

12. The _____ convention was the last major party convention to actually choose a major party candidate for president.
    a. 1992 Democrat
    b. 1976 Republican
    c. 1984 Democrat
    d. 1988 Republican

13. The American political party system is largely _____ centered.
    a. ideology
    b. candidate
    c. issue
    d. party

14. The institutional characteristics of political parties include
    a. parties at the state and local level.
    b. national party leadership.
    c. party platforms.
    d. all of the above.

15. Which of the following elections is most likely to be nonpartisan?
    a. United States senator
    b. state representative
    c. school board
    d. mayoral

PART V — TEST ANSWERS

Pretest

1.	b	6.	d	11.	b
2.	b	7.	a	12.	d
3.	a	8.	a	13.	d
4.	b	9.	a	14.	b
5.	b	10.	b	15.	a

Programmed Review

1. competition
2. slavery
3. party
4. do
5. functions
6. patronage
7. conventions; primaries
8. one
9. candidate; ideology
10. Republican
11. Republican
12. FDR
13. presidential
14. less
15. moderate
16. power
17. federal
18. soft
19. party
20. committee
21. conceal
22. majority
23. more
24. federal
25. closed
26. identification
27. realignment
28. independents
29. issues; organization
30. television
31. national committee
32. superdelegates
33. issue advocacy
34. $10,000

Post-test

1.	c	6.	b	11.	d
2.	c	7.	c	12.	b
3.	d	8.	a	13.	b
4.	c	9.	b	14.	d
5.	c	10.	a	15.	c

Chapter 8
Public Opinion, Participation, and Voting

PART I—LEARNING OBJECTIVES

8.1   What is public opinion?

8.2   What role does public opinion play in American politics?

8.3   How do we acquire our political values and beliefs?

8.4   What is the relationship between social and economic background and political values and beliefs?

8.5   What role has direct citizen participation played in American politics and government?

8.6   What determines who votes and who does not?

8.7   What impact does voting have on government policies and practices?

PART II — PRETEST

1. Nonvoters do *not* have one of the following characteristics:
   a. poor
   b. less educated
   c. less religious
   d. not white

2. Public opinion is best thought of as
   a. the will of the people.
   b. a diversity of opinion within a particular population.
   c. media reflection of public attitudes.
   d. voter attitudes.

3. An institutional barrier that blocks people from voting is
   a. distant voting booths.
   b. registration.
   c. unattractive candidates.
   d. lack of party competition.

4. The group least apt to vote is
   a. 18- to 24-year-olds.
   b. Gray Panthers.
   c. blue-collar workers.
   d. women.

5. The most homogeneous of all groups in molding political opinion is
   a. school.
   b. work.
   c. church membership.
   d. family.

6. Which of the following was most apt to vote Democratic in recent elections?
   a. Jews
   b. blacks
   c. white Protestants
   d. Catholics

7. The major force in the early socialization of children is
    a. television.
    c. school.
    b. family.
    d. playmates.

8. The most influential factor in forming the attitudes of children is
    a. intelligence.
    c. class and race.
    b. psychological and genetic traits.
    d. family and school.

9. Which group tends to be more liberal on both economic/noneconomic issues?
    a. Catholic
    c. atheist
    b. Jewish
    d. Protestant

10. In 2002, both parties were launching major efforts to register/mobilize voters for 2004 from which rapidly growing ethnic or racial group?
    a. Asian Americans
    c. Hispanics
    b. African Americans
    d. Arab Americans

11. Political opinions that exist but have not been fully expressed are referred to as
    a. salience.
    b. intensity.
    c. latency.
    d. random.

12. _____ is the process by which campaigns learn about the issue positions of potential voters.
    a. Canvassing
    b. Focusing
    c. Banking
    d. Petitioning

13. Twenty-five percent of the population is interested in politics most of the time. They are the
    a. attentive public.
    b. core constituents.
    c. smart ones.
    d. public spirited people.

14. The secret ballot printed by the state used to help ensure voter regularity is the
    a. English ballot.
    b. American ballot.
    c. community ballot.
    d. Australian ballot.

15. When a young person's parents and friends disagree on underlying political attitudes such as party affiliation, high school students tend to go along with
    a. friends and peers.
    b. their own independent thinking.
    c. church leaders.
    d. parents.

PART III — PROGRAMMED REVIEW

Knowledge Objective: To consider the complexity of public opinion
1. The people speak with many voices. There is no one set _____.
2. The characteristic of public opinion that measures how strongly people feel on an issue is called _____.
3. _____ attitudes are dormant but may be evoked into action.
4. Opinions which are closely associated with the lives of the individuals are called _____.
5. When a large majority of voters agree on an issue, we have reached _____.
6. When strong opinions are nearly equally divided on an issue, the result is _____.

Knowledge Objective: To examine how we acquire our political attitudes
7. The _____ unit instills the basic attitudes that shape future opinions.
8. The process by which we develop our political attitudes is called political _____.
9. The attitudes of children are shaped by their family _____.
10. After 9/11, many Americans turned their attention to _____ fundamentalism.
11. One should avoid _____ when talking about racial or religious voting.

Knowledge Objective: To examine the practice of "taking the pulse of the people"
12. An accurate poll must be based on a _____ sample of the total universe.
13. Plus or minus 3 percentage points refers to a poll's margin of _____.

Knowledge Objective: To identify those who vote and those who do not
14. The type of political activity most Americans engage in is _____.
15. A subset of the public that has a high level of political interest and awareness is the _____ public.
16. In recent presidential elections, about (half, three-quarters) _____ of potential voters cast ballots.
17. Compared to other nations, voting participation by Americans is (low, high) _____.
18. Millions of Americans fail to vote because they feel there is no real _____.
19. The key factor that determines the degree of voting participation is _____.
20. Persons in the 18-24 age group have the (highest, lowest) _____ voting participation record.
21. Highly educated people are (more, less) _____ apt to vote.
22. The major institutional block to voting is _____.
23. In an effort to attract young voters, Congress passed the _____ law.

24. Nonvoting on the part of the _____ is a part of a larger political-psychological environment that discourages their political activity.
25. The _____ has the greatest influence in determining a person's voting patterns and party allegiance.
26. The best indicator of how a person will vote is _____ identification.
27. More than a third of the voters can be called _____.
28. Recent elections marked a focus from parties to _____.
29. Low-income voters tend to judge a candidate (more, less) _____ on the basis of their own personal financial condition.
30. A person's subjective sense of political identification is called _____.
31. Outranking issues or political ideology is _____ identification.
32. Most presidential candidates (do, do not) _____ clearly define their attitudes on issues.

PART IV — POST-TEST

1. The biggest change in public perception following the terrorist attacks of September 11, 2001 could be found in the increase of Americans now willing to
   a. attend political meetings.
   b. attend church.
   c. trust the national government.
   d. give blood.

2. One of the following is *not* a reason why low-income people vote in fewer numbers.
   a. They have less sense of involvement and confidence.
   b. They feel at a disadvantage in social contacts.
   c. Their social norms tend to deemphasize politics.
   d. They can't afford registration fees.

3. All of the following are true about voter statistics *except*
   a. men out-vote women by a large majority.
   b. middle-aged people are more likely to vote than younger people.
   c. college-educated persons vote more than high school graduates.
   d. persons who are active in organized groups are more likely to vote.

4. An off-year election is one in which
   a. the president is running for reelection.
   b. governors are selected.
   c. senators are selected.
   d. local officials are selected.

5. Candidates with positive appeal include all but
   a. Eisenhower.
   b. Kennedy.
   c. Carter.
   d. Reagan.

6. Voters tend to vote against an incumbent if
   a. the budget is out of balance.
   b. there is an issue conflict.
   c. their personal fortunes are declining.
   d. they have not implemented their campaign promises.

7. Mobilizing voters to vote early in states where it's possible to do so is known as
   a. "assuring the vote."   c. "registering the vote."
   b. "gaining the vote."   d. "banking the vote."

8. Voter registration procedures have been eased by connecting registration to
   a. college registration.   c. a driver's license.
   b. email.   d. W-4 forms.

9. A good public opinion poll does *not* require
   a. qualified interviewers.
   b. carefully phrased questions.
   c. a 25 percent sample of the universe.
   d. a representative sample of the universe.

10. One famous presidential election that the Gallup Poll got wrong was in the year
    a. 1948.   c. 1984.
    b. 1960.   d. 1992.

11. In the Make It Real Visual Literacy feature, the front page of the *Chicago Daily Tribune* in 1948 reports that "_____ Defeats Truman."
    a. Stevenson
    b. Dewey
    c. Roosevelt
    d. Eisenhower

12. _____ is when people will often give a more socially acceptable answer when a truthful response might be somewhat embarrassing.
    a. Halo effect
    b. Confidence interval
    c. Salience
    d. Assumed knowledge

13. The trend in the past few decades seems to indicate that Americans increasingly vote
    a. on issues rather than candidates.
    b. as Independents.
    c. for parties rather than candidates or issues.
    d. for candidates rather than parties.

14. The distribution of individual preferences or evaluation of a given issue, candidate, or institution within a population is called
    a. public opinion.
    b. consensus.
    c. distribution.
    d. individual preference.

15. All of the following are true concerning voter turnout *except*
    a. voter turnout is highest in presidential elections.
    b. voter turnout is higher in general elections than in primary elections.
    c. voter turnout is higher in primary elections than in special elections.
    d. voter turnout is higher in local elections than in national elections.

PART V — TEST ANSWERS

Pretest

1.	c	6.	b	11.	c
2.	b	7.	b	12.	a
3.	b	8.	d	13.	a
4.	a	9.	d	14.	d
5.	d	10.	c	15.	d

Programmed Review

1.	public opinion	17.	low
2.	intensity	18.	choice
3.	Latent	19.	education
4.	salient	20.	lowest
5.	consensus	21.	more
6.	polarization	22.	registration
7.	family	23.	Motor Voter
8.	socialization	24.	poor
9.	environment	25.	family
10.	Islamic	26.	party
11.	stereotypes	27.	independent
12.	random	28.	candidates
13.	error	29.	more
14.	voting	30.	partisanship
15.	attentive	31.	partisan
16.	half	32.	do not

Post-test

1.	c	6.	c	11. b
2.	d	7.	d	12. a
3.	a	8.	c	13. d
4.	d	9.	c	14. a
5.	c	10.	a	15. d

Chapter 9
Campaigns and Elections: Democracy in Action

PART I — LEARNING OBJECTIVES

9.1   What role do elections play in American democracy?
9.2   What rules govern congressional and presidential elections?
9.3   Why are so few congressional elections competitive?
9.4   What is fundraising such an important part of running for office in contemporary America?
9.5   What are the most important consequences of the high cost of state and national political campaigns?
9.6   What suggestions have been made to improve American elections?
9.7   What are the two main phases of a presidential campaign?
9.8   How does campaigning during the primaries differ from campaigning during the general election?
9.9   What trends in voter turnout and enthusiasm have been detected in recent years?

PART II — PRETEST

1. The most important factor in winning a congressional race is
   a. personal contact.
   b. TV time.
   c. press coverage.
   d. money.

2. Recent presidential conventions have been noteworthy because
   a. the winner was known in advance.
   b. major rivals made a down-to-the-wire finish.
   c. excitement ran high.
   d. philosophical differences were deep.

3. The political strength of congressional incumbents has made modern elections
   a. highly competitive.
   b. political party contests.
   c. uncompetitive.
   d. strictly rational contests.

4. The campaign reform law of 1974 was chiefly concerned with
   a. campaign finance.
   b. media coverage.
   c. nomination procedures.
   d. delegate selection.

5. To attain the presidency, a candidate must achieve two goals. These are to
   a. have the largest number of delegates prior to coming to the national convention, and then obtain a majority of the popular vote.
   b. be nominated at the party convention, and obtain a majority of the electoral votes.
   c. be nominated at the party convention, and obtain both a majority of the popular vote and the electoral vote.
   d. be nominated at the party convention, and win a majority of the popular vote.

6. A recent movement for change in the electoral system has pushed for
   a. fixed terms.
   b. staggered terms.
   c. term limitations.
   d. uniform terms.

7. _____ generally benefit more from presidential debates.
   a. Republicans
   b. Challengers
   c. Incumbents
   d. Democrats

8. In the event that no presidential candidate receives a majority of the electoral vote, the president is chosen by
   a. Congress.
   b. the Supreme Court.
   c. the House of Representatives.
   d. the Senate.

9. The 2002 legislation raised the individual contribution limit to each candidate in the general election to _____ dollars.
   a. 4,000
   b. 3,000
   c. 2,000
   d. 1,000

10. The largest expense in recent congressional campaigns has been for
    a. TV-radio advertising.
    b. consultants.
    c. polls.
    d. printing and mailing.

11. Financial contributions by individuals or groups in the hope of influencing the outcome of an election and subsequently influencing policy are labeled
    a. issue money.
    b. soft money.
    c. interested money.
    d .hard money.

12. The method of choosing delegates used by the state of Iowa is a
    a. caucus.
    b. referendum.
    c. primary.
    d. state convention.

13. In recent years, television viewership of presidential nominating conventions has
    a. remained the same.
    b. defied a trend.
    c. increased.
    d. declined.

14. Most election districts in the United States are
    a. multiparty districts.
    b. proportionately distributed districts.
    c. defined by race and class.
    d. single member districts.

15. Which of the following was *not* among the top ten issue advertisers in 2000?
    a. Planned Parenthood
    b. R. J. Reynolds
    c. AFL-CIO
    d. National Rifle Association

PART III — PROGRAMMED PREVIEW

Knowledge Objective: To review the rules for elections
1. Most electoral rules are still matters of _____ law.
2. Federal general elections are the first Tuesday after the first _____ in November of _____ numbered years.
3. Politicians can plan for the next election because we have _____ terms.
4. A recent movement wants to _____ terms of office.
5. Politicians who announce they will not run again are called _____.
6. With our winner-take-all system a winner does not necessarily need to have a _____ of the vote.
7. Proportional representation rewards _____ parties.
8. To win the presidency, the candidate must have a majority vote of the _____.
9. Under the electoral college system, a candidate either wins _____ or _____ of a state's electoral votes.
10. Most states provide for the selection of electors on a (state, district) _____ basis.
11. If no presidential candidate secures a majority of the electoral votes the _____ decides.

Knowledge Objective: To examine the process of running for Congress
12. Competitiveness in congressional elections (has, has not) _____ increased slightly over the past twenty years.
13. Senate elections are likely to be (more, less) _____ competitive than House elections.
14. Congressional candidates whose vote is increased by a strong presidential candidate are said to benefit from the _____ influence.

15. New campaign technology tends to emphasize _____ over issues.
16. Keeping a House seat is (easier, harder) _____ than gaining one.
17. In midterm elections support for the party in power almost always _____.
18. Candidates for Congress secure most of their campaign funds from (the party, personal contributions) _____.
19. Focusing on an opponent's failings is _____ campaigning.

Knowledge Objective: To trace the steps in nominating and electing a president
20. Presidential candidates are now selected by their parties chiefly through the use of _____.
21. When voters in a presidential primary indicate their preference from a list of candidates, the election is commonly referred to as a _____ contest.
22. National conventions normally select a party candidate for president and vice president and write a _____.
23. The party platform is (binding, nonbinding) _____ on the candidate.
24. Nominating conventions provide a time to build party _____.
25. Mistakes made during a presidential debate may damage the candidate's _____.

Knowledge Objective: To study proposed reforms of the electoral college and presidential primaries
26. In caucus states, candidates are less dependent on the _____ and more dependent on their abilities to reach _____ activists.
27. Reform of presidential primaries concentrates on _____ or a _____ primary.
28. The main argument for presidential primaries is that they open up the nomination process to _____ voters.
29. Critics contend the primaries test the candidate for the ability to play the _____.
30. The most common electoral college reform is _____ of the president.

Knowledge Objective: To analyze the sources/uses of money in national campaigns
31. The Keating 5 is an example of the undue influence that comes with large _____.
32. All congressional candidates (are, are not) _____ required to report their campaign contributions and expenditures.
33. FECA election regulations are being undermined by _____ money.
34. The key to congressional campaigns are _____.
35. Organizations and individuals (do, do not) _____ have limitations placed on the amount they may spend independently of a campaign organization.
36. Congressional candidates (do, do not) _____ receive federal campaign funds.
37. The 2002 campaign finance reform law does not constrain _____ expenditures by groups/individuals separately from political candidates.
38. The 1974 campaign reform law achieved a breakthrough by providing for public _____ of presidential campaigns.
39. The 2002 reforms _____ (did, did not) address incumbent fundraising advantages.
40. The 2002 campaign finance reform law bans broadcast ads that show the _____ or _____ of a candidate and occurs in _____ days before a general election.

PART IV — POST-TEST

1. Only one of the following presidential candidates was elected, although each received more popular votes than his opponent.
   - a. Jackson (1824)
   - b. Cleveland (1888)
   - c. Tilden (1876)
   - d. Truman (1948)

2. The bias of the electoral college favors
   - a. one-party states.
   - b. rural areas.
   - c. populous urban states.
   - d. modified one-party states.

3. A state's electoral vote is determined by
   - a. population.
   - b. previous voting patterns in presidential elections.
   - c. a complicated formula devised by Congress.
   - d. the number of its representatives and senators.

4. The Supreme Court voided which of the following provisions of the 1974 campaign reform law?
   - a. limitations on spending
   - b. limitations on giving
   - c. public funding of presidential elections
   - d. election-day registration

5. To be elected president, a candidate must receive
   - a. a plurality of electoral votes.
   - b. a majority of electoral votes.
   - c. a majority of states as well as electoral votes.
   - d. a majority of the popular vote.

6. Most delegates to the national nominating convention are chosen by
   - a. popular votes.
   - b. primary elections.
   - c. state conventions.
   - d. state committees.

7. Presidential candidates are nominated by
   - a. party caucus.
   - b. national party conventions.
   - c. national party committee.
   - d. presidential primary.

8. New candidates for the House of Representatives are normally concerned with
   - a. timing.
   - b. financial support.
   - c. recognition.
   - d. all of the above.

9. The 1974 campaign expense law placed a limit on the contributions that could be made by
   - a. individuals.
   - b. organizations.
   - c. political parties.
   - d. all of the above.

10. A "permanent Congress" is a result of
    a. advantages held by incumbents.   c. redistricting.
    b. direct mail.   d. direct primaries.

11. The 2000 presidential election provides strong evidence that
    a. news networks predict the winners accurately all the time.
    b. someone can lose the popular vote and still win the presidency.
    c. one state's electors do not matter.
    d. the popular vote determines our president.

12. The Bipartisan Campaign Reform Act
    a. abolished the Federal Election Commission.
    b. sets no limit on independent expenditures.
    c. allows the use of corporate and union treasury funds.
    d. established the Federal Election Commission.

13. When a candidate relies on personal contacts, hand shaking, door-to-door campaigning, and seeking positive media attention, he or she is said to be seeking
    a. building a grass-roots foundation.
    b. visibility.
    c. ballot position.
    d. positive reinforcement.

14. The caucus method of selecting a delegate depends largely on
    a. the socio-economic level of a district.
    b. party organization.
    c. grass-roots support for an individual.
    d. financial incentives for an individual candidate.

15. Senate campaigns generally feature all of the following, *except*
    a. millions of dollars spent.
    b. state-of-the-art campaign techniques.
    c. a slight disadvantage for incumbents.
    d. intense competition.

PART V — TEST ANSWERS

Pretest

1.	a	6.	c	11.	c
2.	a	7.	b	12.	a
3.	c	8.	c	13.	d
4.	a	9.	c	14.	d
5.	b	10.	a	15.	b

Programmed Review

1.	state	21.	beauty
2.	Monday; even	22.	platform
3.	fixed	23.	nonbinding
4.	limit	24.	unity
5.	lame duck	25.	credibility
6.	majority	26.	media; political
7.	minority	27.	national; regional
8.	electoral college	28.	more
9.	all; none	29.	media game
10.	state	30.	direct popular election
11.	House of Representatives	31.	contributions
12.	has not	32.	are
13.	more	33.	soft
14.	coattail	34.	PACs
15.	personality	35.	do not
16.	easier	36.	do not
17.	declines	37.	independent
18.	personal contributions	38.	financing
19.	negative	39.	did not
20.	primaries	40.	image; likeness; 60

Post-test

1.	d	6.	b	11.	b
2.	c	7.	b	12.	b
3.	d	8.	d	13.	b
4.	a	9.	d	14.	b
5.	b	10.	a	15.	c

Chapter 10
The Media and American Politics

PART I — LEARNING OBJECTIVES

10.1   What is the mass media?
10.2   How have the media and its role in American society changed over the course of the last century?
10.3   How much power does the media have in contemporary American politics?
10.4   How has media ownership changed in the last several decades?
10.5   What are the most important consequences of recent changes in media ownership?
10.6   What is the relationship between the media and public political debate?
10.7   What role does the media play in shaping campaigns and elections?
10.8   How does the government regulate the media?
10.9   What limits are there on freedom of the press?
10.10   What is the relationship between the media and politicians?

PART II — PRETEST

1. Freedom of the press is guaranteed by
    a. American tradition.
    b. common law.
    c. Congress.
    d. a constitutional amendment.

2. One of the following media powers is normally *not* included in the top national ranking.
    a. *Reader's Digest*
    b. *ABC*
    c. *Wall Street Journal*
    d. *USA Today*

3. The media's new form of a town meeting is
    a. *60 Minutes*.
    b. computer voting.
    c. Web chat rooms.
    d. soundbites.

4. The network semi-monopoly over television has been _____ by C-SPAN and CNN.
   a. reinforced
   b. diminished
   c. untouched
   d. overshadowed

5. The media during a presidential election tend not to stress
   a. issues.
   b. personalities.
   c. strategy.
   d. the race.

6. Recent studies of the media's political reporting tend to be critical of their
   a. partisan bias.
   b. skimpy political coverage.
   c. repetitive coverage of issues.
   d. treatment of the election as a contest.

7. Which of the following has *not* become a national newspaper?
   a. *Atlanta Constitution*
   b. *USA Today*
   c. *The Wall Street Journal*
   d. *The New York Times*

8. The most trusted source of news is
   a. newspapers.
   b. news magazines.
   c. radio.
   d. television.

9. The president who had been most successful in using television to further his goals was
   a. Kennedy.
   b. Eisenhower.
   c. Franklin Roosevelt.
   d. Reagan.

10. The mass media's impact on most Americans is modified by their
    a. regionalism.
    b. viewing habits.
    c. lack of background.
    d. selective perception.

11. The most important factor in political socialization for the American public is
    a. radio.
    b. a combination of radio and television.
    c. television.
    d. the family.

12. Which president most enjoyed matching wits with confrontational reporters?
    a. Kennedy
    b. George W. Bush
    c. Reagan
    d. Clinton

13. With cable television came
    a. less trained reporters.
    b. round-the-clock news coverage.
    c. less news on network news programs.
    d. less of a reliance on television for news.

14. The Gannett Corporation is an example of
    a. adversarial journalism.
    b. indirect government ownership of the press.
    c. advocacy journalism.
    d. a media conglomerate.

15. Which news medium was most responsible for exposing the average American to the injustice done to blacks during the Civil Rights Movement?
    a. newspapers
    b. radio
    c. television
    d. Internet

PART III — PROGRAMMED REVIEW

Knowledge Objective: To evaluate the power of the mass media
1. In modern America the mass media is so powerful that it is sometimes called the _____ of government.
2. Recent expansion of news sources has resulted in more competition for _____.
3. The _____ media is the part of the mass media that stresses the news.
4. The early American press served as a political _____ for political leaders.
5. Professional journalists believe the journalists should be _____ of partisan politics.
6. FDR effectively used the radio to _____ the editorial screening of the press.

7. Today _____ is the most important source of news for most Americans.
8. Media conglomerates now dominate the media business and have contributed to the _____ of news.
9. Critics charge that information today is more diluted and moderated because local TV and newspapers are not owned by _____ firms.
10. The _____ , not political parties, are now judging candidates in terms of character.

Knowledge Objective: To examine the relationship of the media and public opinion
11. For a long time political scientists have tended to (stress, play down) _____ the mass media's political influence.
12. Defense mechanisms such as _____ perception modify the influence of the mass media.
13. A powerful check on media as an opinion-making force is _____.
14. Much of the media's opinion-making role is (direct, indirect) _____.
15. The final decision in determining the public agenda (is, is not) _____ made by the media.
16. _____ complain that the media are too liberal, and the liberals claim the media are too _____.
17. David Broder has expressed concern about the _____ of journalists who previously were in government service.
18. Modern presidents have turned away from the press and to _____ and _____ to communicate with the public.
19. In recent decades, newspaper publishers tended to support _____ presidential candidates.
20. Generally, reporters are _____, while publishers take _____ positions.
21. Critics of presidential use of television have called TV a _____.
22. Some critics contend that elite journalists have a _____ bias.
23. Some studies indicate that the liberal bias of reporters (is, is not) _____ reflected in their on-the-job performance.

Knowledge Objective: To evaluate the role of the media in elections
24. The media tend to portray the presidential election as a _____.
25. Public relations experts attached to campaigns tend to stress the candidate's _____.
26. Election experts tend to determine their campaign strategy on the basis of _____.
27. Old-time party leaders have been replaced in presidential campaigns by experts and _____.
28. The broadcast networks now attract only about _____ percent of the viewing public.

Knowledge Objective: To evaluate media power in American politics

29. The press does not pay much attention to policy _____.
30. In evaluating media power, the media scholars (agree, disagree) _____.
31. The news media's greatest role as a participant is probably at the _____ level of government.
32. Lack of coverage of the bureaucracy is due to little interest by the media in reporting policy _____.
33. Most media coverage of Congress is its reaction to initiatives of the _____.
34. Most Americans believe that the media (is, is not) _____ a valuable watchdog over government.

PART IV — POST-TEST

1. In most national elections a majority of newspapers endorse _____ candidates.
   a. conservative
   b. liberal
   c. independent
   d. no

2. Critics of media employees charge that an overwhelming majority are
   a. conservative.
   b. liberal.
   c. independent.
   d. apolitical.

3. The most influential component of today's mass media is
   a. newspapers.
   b. television.
   c. radio.
   d. news magazines

4. In addition to their public service role in providing information, the media also
   a. are privately owned.
   b. are big business.
   c. stress profits.
   d. are all of the above.

5. The modern president who had held the fewest news conferences was
   a. Carter.
   b. Reagan.
   c. Nixon.
   d. Johnson.

6. Using entertainment techniques to present the news is called
   a. infotainment.
   b. Internet.
   c. a media event.
   d. an infomercial.

7. Ownership of media outlets is
   a. widely dispersed.
   b. concentrated.
   c. unprofitable.
   d. family-oriented.

8. The president who held the largest number of press conferences was
   a. John F. Kennedy.
   b. Franklin D. Roosevelt.
   c. Richard M. Nixon.
   d. Lyndon B. Johnson.

9. How citizens interpret information from politicians depends upon all but
   a. recall ability.
   b. political socialization.
   c. hours spent watching television.
   d. selectivity.

10. The institution least dependent on the press is the
    a. Supreme Court.
    b. president.
    c. bureaucracy.
    d. Congress.

11. Conglomerate ownership of American communication assets includes all *except*
    a. the Public Broadcasting Corporation.
    b. *The Chicago Tribune.*
    c. the Gannett Corporation.
    d. the News Corporation.

12. When individuals screen out those messages that do not conform to their own biases, they are said to be practicing
    a. selective exposure.
    b. perception.
    c. viewing.
    d. rights.

13. In 2002, over 40 percent of Republicans believed all or most of what came from
    a. *The Wall Street Journal.*
    b. CNN.
    c. MSNBC.
    d. Fox News.

14. News coverage of Congress, compared to coverage of the president, tends to be
    a. more issue oriented.
    b. more objective than coverage of the president.
    c. more positive.
    d. more negative.

15. More than half of Americans say they are regular viewers of
    a the evening network news programs.
    b. local news programs.
    c. *60 Minutes.*
    d. CNN, CNBC, MSNBC, or Fox News.

PART V — TEST ANSWERS

Pretest

1.	d	6.	d	11.	d
2.	a	7.	a	12.	d
3.	c	8.	d	13.	b
4.	b	9.	d	14.	d
5.	a	10.	d	15.	c

Programmed Review

1. fourth branch
2. newspapers
3. news
4. mouthpiece
5. independent
6. bypass
7. television
8. centralization
9. local
10. press
11. play down
12. selective
13. group affiliation
14. indirect
15. is not
16. Conservatives; pro-establishment
17. objectivity
18. radio; television
19. Republican
20. liberal; conservative
21. throne
22. cultural
23. is not
24. race
25. image
26. soundbites
27. consultants
28. 40
29. implementation
30. disagree
31. local
32. implementation
33. president
34. is

Post-test

1.	a	6.	a	11.	a
2.	b	7.	b	12.	a
3.	b	8.	b	13.	a
4.	d	9.	c	14.	d
5.	c	10.	a	15.	d

Chapter 11
Congress: The People's Branch

PART I — LEARNING OBJECTIVES

11.1   What are the most important powers of Congress?
11.2   How are congressional districts drawn?
11.3   Who controls the apportionment and redistricting process?
11.4   Who gets elected to Congress and why?
11.5   What are the jobs of the federal legislator?
11.6   Who do legislators represent?
11.7   How is the legislative branch of the federal government organized?
11.8   How do bills become laws?
11.9   How are congressional ethics and norms defined?
11.10 What are the possible consequences of violating congressional rules?
11.11 Why is it often so difficult for Congress to act quickly and decisively?

PART II — PRETEST

1. All of the following are true about the House of Representatives *except*
    a. legislators in the House have two-year terms.
    b. there are 435 members in the House.
    c. policy specialists are common in the House.
    d. a filibuster is common in the House.

2. Gerrymandering occurs when the majority party
    a. supports benefits for blue-collar workers.
    b. promises to promote legislation for certain districts.
    c. draws district lines to win as many districts as possible.
    d. draws district lines to maximize its popular vote.

3. Authorization of a program by Congress means nothing until
    a. OMB submits a budget.
    b. the Rules Committee reaches agreement.
    c. the legislative session ends.
    d. Congress appropriates funds.

4. The chief responsibility of congressional staff is to
   a. handle constituent mail.
   b. serve as receptionists.
   c. schedule office appointments.
   d. advise on legislation.

5. Congress does *not* perform one of these functions.
   a. policy clarification
   b. consensus building
   c. foreign policy initiatives
   d. lawmaking

6. The Speaker of the House of Representatives does all of the following *except*
   a. grants recognition to a member.
   b. appoints select and conference committees.
   c. controls committee assignments.
   d. directs general business on the floor.

7. In the Senate, the committee responsible for each party's overall legislative program is called the _____ committee.
   a. policy
   b. direction
   c. strategy
   d. ways-and-means

8. Legislators who base their votes on their analysis of the long-run welfare of the nation are playing a _____ role.
   a. delegate
   b. trustee
   c. pragmatic
   d. pollster's

9. The seniority system is respected for *all but one* of the following reasons:
   a. encourages members to stay on a committee
   b. encourages expertise
   c. assures aggressiveness and risk taking
   d. reduces interpersonal politics

10. With 55 votes in the Senate, the Republicans still fall _____ short of the number needed to shut down filibusters.
    a. ten
    b. fifteen
    c. one
    d. five

11. Which of the following is *not* a function of a party caucus?
    a. approve committee assignment
    b. elect party officers
    c. pass legislation
    d. veto legislation

12. Incumbents are generally reelected because they
    a. have high name recognition.
    b. have greater access to the media.
    c. can raise more campaign money.
    d. all of the above

13. If a district is predictably won by one party, it is called a
    a. party district.
    b. safe seat.
    c. candidate's dream.
    d. sure bet.

14. Members of Congress are assigned to committees by the
    a. Steering and Policy Committee.
    b. Committee on Committees.
    c. Speaker of the House and president pro tempore of the Senate.
    d. both a and b

15. Through effective use of their constitutional and political powers, presidents are usually
    a. partners with Congress in the legislative process.
    b. involved in too many other affairs to worry about the legislative process.
    c. in strong opposition to Congress in the legislative process.
    d. not willing to work with Congress in the legislative process.

PART III — PROGRAMMED REVIEW

Knowledge Objective: To review the system for election to Congress and to profile those elected
1. Redrawing the district lines of U.S. representatives after each census is the responsibility of _____.
2. _____ is the process of drawing electoral boundaries to maximize the majority party's House majority.
3. Being an incumbent is a(n) _____ for a member of Congress seeking reelection.
4. In 1995 the Supreme Court ruled that making race "the predominant factor" while ignoring traditional principles was _____.
5. A _____ seat is one that is predictably won by one party.
6. Nearly half of the legislators are _____ by profession.

Knowledge Objective: To analyze the structure and powers of the houses of Congress
7. The framers designed the _____ to reflect the popular will and the _____ to provide stability.
8. The _____ holds the place in government the framers intended for Congress.
9. Congress has the power to declare _____.
10. The Senate is chaired by a _____ in the absence of the vice president.

72

11. Assisting each floor leader are the party _____ who serve as liaisons between the House leadership and the rank-and-file members.
12. In the Senate, each party has a(n) _____ which is in theory responsible for the party's overall legislative program.
13. The tradition of submitting names of appointees to the senator from the state where the appointee resides is called _____.
14. A filibuster in the Senate can be shut off only by a(n) _____ vote.
15. The Senate has the power to _____ presidential nominations.

Knowledge Objective: To consider the job of the legislator
16. Members of Congress who see their role as _____ believe they should serve the "folks back home."
17. Members of Congress who see their role as _____ are free-thinking legislators who vote their conscience.
18. The main influence on legislators is their perception of how their _____ feel about the matters brought before Congress.
19. Most members of Congress are now highly dependent on their _____ .

Knowledge Objective: To trace the lawmaking process
20. From the very beginning, Congress has been a system of multiple _____ .
21. To follow a bill through the congressional labyrinth is to see the _____ of power in Congress.
22. Proponents of new legislation must win at every step; _____ need win only once.

Knowledge Objective: To examine the committee system
23. All bills introduced in the House are sent to _____ committees.
24. As the power of congressional subcommittees has expanded, the importance of _____ has diminished.
25. _____ are still usually named on the basis of seniority.
26. If neither house will accept the other's bills, a(n) _____ settles the difference.

PART IV — POST-TEST

1. The profile of the 108th Congress would tend to support which assertion?
   a. The vast majority were men.
   b. There were no women.
   c. The average age was 35-40.
   d. It was racially and ethnically diverse.

2. Members of Congress from competitive districts are apt to make _____ their first priority.
   a. serving the home folks
   b. foreign policy
   c. national issues
   d. supporting the president

3. Special responsibilities of the Senate *do not include* two of the following:
   a. ratification of treaties
   b. confirmation of presidential nominees
   c. a final veto on appropriations
   d. nomination of ambassadors to foreign countries

4. In terms of the general makeup of Congress, which of the following people would be most typical?
   a. a millionaire Jewish stockbroker
   b. a Catholic steel worker
   c. a Protestant female elementary teacher
   d. a middle-income male lawyer

5. One of the following persons would have the best chance of election to Congress:
   a. an incumbent representative
   b. a popular TV anchorperson
   c. an experienced state legislator
   d. a famous woman astronaut

6. Free-thinking and independent legislators see their role as
   a. national figures.
   b. trustees.
   c. diplomats.
   d. ambassadors from localities.

7. The role of the president has become enhanced at the expense of the Congress, especially _____ policy.
   a. domestic
   b. foreign
   c. economic
   d. social

8. The vast majority of the bills introduced every two years in both chambers are
   a. passed.
   b. still under debate.
   c. killed.
   d. withdrawn.

9. The majority floor leader is an officer
   a. only of his party.
   b. in charge of both parties in standing and conference committees.
   c. in charge of both parties on the floor.
   d. who presides over the Senate.

10. House party whips do all of the following *except*
    a. serve as liaison between leadership and the rank-and-file.
    b. inform members when important bills will be voted.
    c. lobby strongly for support of the majority leader.
    d. try to ensure maximum attendance for critical votes.

11. If Congress has adjourned and the president waits ten days without signing a bill, it
    a. can be amended by the president without congressional approval.
    b. must be referred back to the next session of Congress.
    c. passes without his signature.
    d. is a pocket veto.

12. A(n) _____, if signed by a majority of the members of the House of Representatives, will pry a bill from committee and bring it to the floor for consideration.
    a. pocket veto
    b. discharge petition
    c. rider
    d. override

13. The drawing of legislative district boundaries to benefit a party, group, or incumbent is known as
    a. gerrymandering.
    b. reapportionment.
    c. redistricting.
    d. redlining.

14. The right to unlimited debate
    a. can be subject to cloture.
    b. is found in the Senate but not the House.
    c. is called the "filibuster."
    d. all of the above

15. An official who is expected to represent the views of his or her constituents even when personally holding different views is known as a
    a. candidate.
    b. politician.
    c. delegate.
    d. trustee.

PART V — TEST ANSWERS

Pretest

1.	d	6.	c	11.	c
2.	c	7.	a	12.	d
3.	d	8.	b	13.	b
4.	d	9.	c	14.	d
5.	c	10.	d	15.	a

Programmed Review

1. state legislatures
2. Gerrymandering
3. advantage
4. unconstitutional
5. safe
6. lawyers
7. House; Senate
8. president
9. war
10. president pro tempore
11. whips
12. policy committee
13. senatorial courtesy
14. cloture
15. confirm
16. delegate
17. trustee
18. constituents
19. staff
20. vetoes
21. dispersion
22. opponents
23. standing
24. seniority
25. Chairpersons
26. conference committee

Post-test

1. a
2. a
3. c
4. d
5. a
6. b
7. b
8. c
9. a
10. c
11. d
12. b
13. a
14. d
15. c

Chapter 12
The Presidency: The Leadership Branch

PART I — LEARNING OBJECTIVES

12.1   What are the formal and informal powers of the president?
12.2   How has the office of the president changed over the course of American history?
12.3   What are the most important recent trends affecting the power and role of the executive branch in American government?
12.4   What makes a great president?
12.5   How is the executive branch organized?
12.6   What role does the president play in contemporary American government?
12.7   What part does the president play in the legislative process?
12.8   What role does Congress play in oversight of the executive branch?

PART II — PRETEST

1. Critics of the presidency seldom charge that it is a(n) _____ institution.
    a.   remote, aristocratic
    b.   weak, flabby
    c.   status quo
    d.   Establishment

2. Only one of the following presidents is apt to appear on a list of "greats."
    a.   Buchanan
    b.   Grant
    c.   Truman
    d.   Harding

3. The framers of the Constitution did *not* anticipate presidential
    a.   symbolic functions.
    b.   abuses of power.
    c.   magisterial functions.
    d.   legislative role.

4. The Supreme Court decision in *Curtiss v. Wright* (1936) upheld strong presidential authority over
    a.   foreign policy.
    b.   domestic policy.
    c.   budget.
    d.   appointments.

5. The constitutionally required age for a president is
   a. 35.
   b. 40.
   c. 45.
   d. 50.

6. The important central presidential staff agency that advises the president about hundreds of government agencies is the
   a. Office of Oversight and Investigation.
   b. CIA.
   c. Office of Management and Budget.
   d. GAO.

7. The vice president has *not* normally been used by modern presidents to
   a. chair advisory councils.
   b. execute day-to-day policy.
   c. undertake goodwill missions.
   d. serve as a senior advisor.

8. The following persisting paradoxes of the American presidency are true *except* that a president should be
   a. programmatic, but a pragmatic and flexible leader.
   b. a common person who can give an uncommon performance.
   c. a person who delivers more than he or she promises.
   d. above politics, yet a skilled political coalition builder.

9. The fundamental power of the president that can be used to accomplish his goals is
   a. artful deception.
   b. persuasion.
   c. outright deceit.
   d. partisanship.

10. The cabinet secretary who would be last in line to become president handles the Department of
    a. State.
    b. Labor.
    c. Homeland Security.
    d. Defense.

11. The _____ has/have been used to acquire Louisiana and during the Civil War to impose a blockade of Confederate shipping.
    a. enlisted powers
    b. take care clause
    c. supremacy clause
    d. inherent powers

12. Which of the following is *not* a precedent established by President Washington?
    a. appointed department secretaries
    b. assembled the first White House Staff
    c. constitutional amendment to restrict the president to two terms
    d. negotiated treaties

13. Which of the following statements is *not* correct regarding the Mexican presidency?
    a. The Mexican legislature and judiciary can check the presidency.
    b. The Mexican president is one of the most powerful executives in the democratic world.
    c. The president serves without a vice president.
    d. The president can serve only one six-year term.

14. Kerry won the state of _____ which Bush won in 2000.
    a. New Hampshire
    b. Florida
    c. Iowa
    d. Ohio

15. President _____ was viewed in a lesser light while in office but was later recognized as great.
    a. Washington
    b. Coolidge
    c. Hoover
    d. Grant

PART III — PROGRAMMED REVIEW

Knowledge Objective: To analyze the characteristics that Americans expect of their president
   1. The framers of the Constitution both _____ and _____ centralized leadership.
   2. The central characteristic that Americans demand of their president is the quality of _____.
   3. In judging presidents, voters rate _____ and _____ over policy decisions.
   4. Active presidents are sometimes accused of being _____.

Knowledge Objective: To examine the president's constitutional position
   5. The framers created a presidency of _____ powers.
   6. The president's power is limited by a system of _____ and _____.
   7. The president must be a _____ citizen.
   8. Great Britain has a _____ system.

Knowledge Objective: The challenging job of being president and vice president
   9. The principle of _____ control over the military is inherent in U.S. democracy.
   10. The Ethics in Government Act requires _____ of _____ requirements.

11. Even since the _____, presidents are expected to keep unemployment low.
12. The vice president casts a tie-breaking vote if there is a tie in the _____.
13. Presidents must build _____ in order to get the agreement of diverse groups.
14. Presidents use State of the _____ Addresses.
15. Presidents use a _____ and _____ organization.

Knowledge Objective: To analyze symbolic leadership
16. The president's power has been greatly increased by the mass media, especially _____.
17. The swelling of the presidency in part results from the _____ expectations.
18. Presidents face a conflict between their role as chief of state and their role as _____ leader.
19. In acting for all the people, the president is a symbolic leader and _____ of state.

Knowledge Objective: To examine the presidential establishment, constraints on the president, and the issue of presidential accountability
20. The Supreme Court in the *Curtiss v. Wright* case decided that the president (did, did not) _____ have exclusive powers in the field of international relations.
21. Since presidents appoint thousands of top officials, one of the chief presidential duties is _____.
22. Bill Clinton's wife and first lady was the policy activist _____.
23. For economic policy the president depends on the Secretary of the Treasury, the Council of Economic Advisers, and the Director of the _____.
24. A president who is a successful leader knows where the _____ are.
25. George W. Bush relies heavily on his vice president, Dick _____.
26. To influence media coverage, the president holds _____ .
27. To gauge public opinion, presidents commission private _____ .
28. An effective president uses political parties (more, less) _____.
29. In recent years presidents have come to rely heavily on their personal _____.
30. The Office of _____ and _____ continues to be the central presidential staff agency.
31. Presidents seldom turn to the _____ as a collective body for advice.
32. The vice president could serve as "Acting President" under the _____ Amendment.
33. Australia and Israel have _____ forms of government.
34. The modern media is the number one _____ of the presidency.
35. The American people regard television as (more, less) _____ trustworthy than most other American institutions.

Knowledge Objective: To understand ideas underlying congressional-presidential relations
36. _____ support is crucial to a president's success with Congress.
37. Appointing the friends and political supporters of key members of Congress to various federal positions is called _____.
38. Kennedy, Reagan, and Clinton were considered _____ (effective, ineffective) communicators.
39. The "genius" of Congress is deliberation, debate, and _____.

40. The two types of resources that shape a president's agenda are _____ and
_____.

PART IV — POST-TEST

1. The American public today gives priority to one aspect of the president.
   a. leadership
   b. honesty
   c. wisdom
   d. policy positions

2. Presidents have the most leeway in
   a. foreign and military affairs.
   b. domestic appropriation matters.
   c. budget appropriations.
   d. social policy.

3. Often a president's "new initiatives" in domestic policy are
   a. highly creative.
   b. previously considered in Congress.
   c. previously thought of by past presidents.
   d. a response to grassroots demands.

4. The functions of the White House staff include *all but*
   a. domestic policy.
   b. economic policy.
   c. congressional relations.
   d. intelligence operations.

5. If the president is to be a successful politician, he must be able to
   a. give commands.
   b. manage conflict.
   c. stand on principles.
   d. rise above politics.

6. Modern presidential cabinets as a collective body have been used by presidents
   a. as high-level advisers.
   b. to create a quasi-parliamentary system.
   c. very infrequently.
   d. to assess new policy proposals.

7. Which amendment limits the president to two terms in office?
   a. Twentieth.
   b. Twenty-Second.
   c. Twenty-Fifth.
   d. Twenty-Seventh

8. Which president was told by the Supreme Court to release steel mills from federal control?
   a. Truman
   b. Nixon
   c. Eisenhower
   d. Carter

9. Presidents who enter office with a large electoral margin, high public approval, and a party majority in Congress often claim a(n) _____ to govern.
   a. rule
   b. mandate
   c. authority
   d. absolute power

10. Which of the following is usually ranked as one of the "ten best" presidents?
    a. Nixon
    b. Coolidge
    c. Eisenhower
    d. Grant

11. Which is correct regarding ways a bill can become law?
    a. The president can sign a bill into law.
    b. A bill can become law if Congress passes it, adjourns, and the president takes no action at all.
    c. Congress can override a presidential veto.
    d. The president can use a line item veto.

12. The Constitutional Convention never seriously considered selection of the president by
    a. the legislative branch.
    b. the Electoral College.
    c. direct election.
    d. the Congress.

13. At the top of the list of what people want to know about their presidential candidates is
    a. the candidate's ability to connect with people.
    b. the candidate's personal finances.
    c. the candidate's church involvement.
    d. whether or not the candidate has a reputation for honesty.

14. In *United States v. Carolene Products* (1936), the Supreme Court granted to the president virtually complete power to
    a. conduct foreign relations.
    b. run the military.
    c. pardon criminals.
    d. none of the above

15. The executive power of the presidency includes all of the following *except* the power
    a. to develop recommendations for spending money.
    b. to oversee the bureaucracy.
    c. to declare war.
    d. to select the senior appointees of government.

PART V — TEST ANSWERS

Pretest

1.	b	6.	c	11.	d
2.	c	7.	b	12.	c
3.	a	8.	c	13.	a
4.	a	9.	b	14.	a
5.	a	10.	c	15.	a

Programmed Review

1. admired; feared
2. leadership
3. character; integrity
4. dictators
5. limited
6. checks; balances
7. natural-born
8. parliamentary
9. civilian
10. conflict; interest
11. New Deal
12. Senate
13. coalition
14. Union
15. line; staff
16. television
17. public's
18. party
19. chief
20. did
21. recruitment
22. Hillary Clinton
23. OMB
24. followers
25. Cheney
26. press conferences
27. opinion polls
28. more
29. staff
30. Management; Budget
31. cabinet
32. Twenty-Fifth
33. parliamentary
34. adversary
35. more
36. Public
37. patronage
38. effective
39. reflection
40. political; decision making

Post-test

1. a
2. a
3. b
4. d
5. b
6. c
7. b
8. a
9. b
10. c
11. d
12. c
13. d
14. d
15. c

Chapter 13
The Federal Administrative System: Executing the Laws

PART I — LEARNING OBJECTIVES

13.1   What is a bureaucracy?

13.2   Why do bureaucracies have such a bad reputation?

13.3   How is the federal bureaucracy organized?

13.4   How much control does the president have over the organization and operation of the federal bureaucracy?

13.5   What are the most important responsibilities of the federal bureaucracy?

13.6   How are positions in the federal bureaucracy filled?

13.7   What role do political leaders play in staffing the federal bureaucracy?

13.8   To whom is the federal bureaucracy accountable?

13.9   How do political pressures shape the organization, actions, and policies of the federal bureaucracy?

13.10 How do bureaucratic realities shape the policy choices of political leaders?

13.11 How have the responsibilities of the federal bureaucracy changed in recent years?

13.12 What constraints are there on the actions and policies of the federal bureaucracy?

PART II — PRETEST

1. Depending on the observer, red tape can be described in *all but one* of the following ways:
    a. an inevitability of government
    b. civil service employees who serve under the merit system
    c. rigid procedures
    d. a bureaucracy that is more interested in means than ends

2. Nearly 25 percent of all civilian employees of the federal government work for
    a. defense agencies.
    b. the Social Security Administration.
    c. welfare agencies.
    d. the Interstate Commerce Commission.

3. Most independent agencies of government are created by
    a. the president.   c. the cabinet.
    b. Congress   d. none of the above.

4. An example of a government corporation is
    a. Securities and Exchange Commission.
    b. U.S. Mint.
    c. Government Printing Office.
    d. FDIC.

5. Independent regulatory boards have *all but one* of these special characteristics.
    a. They do not report directly to the president.
    b. They perform legislative functions.
    c. Their members are political appointees whose terms coincide with the president's.
    d. They have judicial functions.

6. A landmark law creating a merit system of civil service was the congressional act named for its sponsor.
    a. Garfield
    b. Sedman
    c. Pendleton
    d. Hatch

7. The OPM plays *all but one* of the following roles in recruiting new civil service employees.
    a. administers and scores tests
    b. designates the individual an agency must hire
    c. creates a ranked register of successful applicants
    d. certifies three names for each agency vacancy

8. The Hatch Act provides that government employees can do all *except*
    a. make campaign contributions.
    b. attend political rallies.
    c. assist in voter registration.
    d. sell political fund-raising tickets to subordinates.

9. The General Services Administration best exemplifies a(an)
    a. independent agency.
    b. independent regulatory board.
    c. government corporation.
    d. bureau.

10. The weakest relationship of most federal administrators is with
    a. fellow colleagues.
    b. lobbyists.
    c. congressional committees.
    d. the president.

11. Which of the following is *not* one of the key decisions made by the framers about who would be responsible for executing the laws?
    a. decided not to give Congress the power to appoint the treasurer
    b. directed the president of the Senate to oversee the bureaucracy
    c. prohibited members of the House and Senate from holding executive offices
    d. none of the above

12. In 2002 the U.S. Postal Service
    a. lost $3 billion.
    b. profited $3 billion.
    c. profited $1.5 billion.
    d. lost $1.5 billion.

13. Which department does not call its chief administrator the Secretary of the department?
    a. Homeland Security
    b. Defense
    c. State
    d. Justice

14. A _____ is usually the largest organization in government, and is also the highest rank in the federal hierarchy.
    a. division
    b. bureau
    c. cabinet
    d. department

15. The term "bureaucracy" originally referred to
    a. a person's clothing bureau with specific drawers.
    b. the cloth covering the flat writing tables of the French government.
    c. the top to bottom ordering of Russian government officials.
    d. a selective method of hierarchical hiring.

PART III — PROGRAMMED REVIEW

Knowledge Objective: To examine the shape of federal bureaucracy
1. The bureaucracy consists of _____ cabinet-level departments.
2. Nearly _____ percent of all federal civilian employees work for the defense agencies.
3. Bureaucracy originally referred to a _____, _____ method of organization.
4. Most federal employees are _____-collar workers.
5. The federal level of bureaucracy has (grown, decreased) _____ in the past few years.
6. Federal employees are _____ (more, less) representative of the nation as a whole than legislators.

7. The common basis for organization of a department is _____ .
8. An example of a government _____ is the Corporation for Public Broadcasting.
9. A weak link in the bureaucracy are the _____ secretaries.

Knowledge Objective: To trace the evolution of the U.S. Civil Service
10. The _____ system permitted newly elected presidents to appoint their supporters.
11. Restrictions on the political activities of federal employees were imposed by the _____ Act.
12. Federal employees (may, may not) _____ take an active part in partisan politics.
13. The IRS only audits _____ people a year.
14. After a bill becomes law, bureaucrats must be concerned with the law being _____.

Knowledge Objective: To analyze the public's view of bureaucracy
15. Most Americans support bureaucracy that operates in their interest while being critical of big bureaucracy in the _____ .
16. Critics contend a central problem with bureaucracy is our failure to _____ and _____ it.
17. About _____ of federal employees have joined unions.
18. The _____ of a federal agency is the _____ rather than the rule.
19. An _____ agency is not tied to any of the three branches.
20. The complex rules and regulations under which bureaucracy functions is called _____.
21. The process of contracting out public services to private organizations is called _____ .

Knowledge Objective: To discover the controls under which bureaucrats operate
22. Major control of bureaucracy is shared by _____ and the _____ .
23. The Civil Service Reform Act (1978) created a top grade of career bureaucrats, the _____ .
24. Supporters of the patronage system believe that the existing _____ system of federal employment encourages dead wood.
25. _____ is the executive office responsible for managing the federal bureaucracy.
26. The responsiveness of bureaucrats is limited by the procedures that make them _____ .

PART IV — POST-TEST

1. The largest subunit of a government department is usually called a
   a. bureau.
   b. division.
   c. commission.
   d. cabin.

87

2. Presidents like to reorganize the bureaucracy because
   a. managerial controls can be increased.
   b. priorities can be symbolized.
   c. policy integration can be improved.
   d. all of the above

3. Congress normally controls the bureaucracy in all of the following ways *except*
   a. budgetary appropriation.
   b. holding hearings.
   c. confirmation of personnel.
   d. firing civil servants.

4. Between 2000 and 2003, the size of the federal bureaucracy
   a. grew by nearly 500,000 employees.
   b. grew by nearly 100,000 employees.
   c. shrunk by nearly 500,000 employees.
   d. shrunk by nearly 100,000 employees.

5. An example of informal organization would be when a superior and his subordinates
   a. hunt and fish together.
   b. confer over bureau policy.
   c. jointly evaluate employees for promotion.
   d. establish long-range budget plans.

6. Who controls the bureaucracy?
   a. the president
   b. Congress
   c. no single power
   d. the voter

7. In practice the Senior Executive Service has
   a. been successful.
   b. been a failure.
   c. had little impact.
   d. transformed the Civil Service.

8. An effective device for implementing the president's wishes is the
   a. Senior Executive Service.
   b. Office of Management and Budget.
   c. Civil Service Reform Act.
   d. Assistant Secretaries.

9. The responsiveness of a bureaucracy is closely linked to its
    a. accountability.
    b. security.
    c. clientele.
    d. computer capability.

10. Privatization is:
    a. the commissioning of merchant ships as a part of the navy.
    b. secrecy of interoffice memos.
    c. president's right to withhold his IRS return.
    d. placing certain government functions in the private sector.

11. Only about _____ of the federal career civilian employees work in the Washington, D.C. area.
    a. 28 percent
    b. 33 percent
    c. 8 percent
    d. 15 percent

12. Which agency hears charges of wrongdoing and orders corrective and disciplinary action against executive employees or agencies when necessary?
    a. Civil Service Commission
    b. Office of Personnel Management
    c. Merit Systems Protection Board
    d. Office of Management and Budget

13. A career government employee is known as a(n)
    a. representative.
    b. bureaucrat.
    c. fed.
    d. insider.

14. Which of the following functions of government uses the most employees?
    a. Postal Service
    b. Welfare
    c. Correction
    d. Streets and Highways

15. Which department was most recently added to the executive branch?
    a. Department of Homeland Security
    b. Department of Veterans Affairs
    c. Department of Education
    d. Department of Justice

PART V — TEST ANSWERS

Pretest

1.	b	6.	c	11.	b
2.	a	7.	b	12.	b
3.	b	8.	d	13.	d
4.	d	9.	a	14.	d
5.	c	10.	d	15.	b

Programmed Review

1.	fourteen	15.	abstract
2.	25	16.	control; discipline
3.	rational, efficient	17.	one-third
4.	white	18.	death; exception
5.	decreased	19.	independent
6.	more	20.	red tape
7.	function	21.	privatization
8.	corporation	22.	Congress; president
9.	assistant	23.	Senior Executive Service
10.	spoils	24.	tenure
11.	Hatch	25.	OMB
12.	may not	26.	accountable
13.	2 million		
14.	implemented		

Post-test

1.	a	6.	c	11.	d
2.	d	7.	c	12.	c
3.	d	8.	b	13.	b
4.	b	9.	a	14.	a
5.	a	10.	d	15.	a

Chapter 14
The Judiciary: The Balancing Branch

PART I — LEARNING OBJECTIVES

14.1   What role does the federal judicial system play in contemporary American government?
14.2   What is "judicial activism"?
14.3   How is the federal judicial system organized?
14.4   What limits are there on the interpretation of the law and the Constitution by federal judges?
14.5   What powers do judges have to ensure that their rulings are enforced?
14.6   Has the process of selecting federal judges become too "politicized"?
14.7   How are federal judges selected?
14.8   What role does the Supreme Court play in contemporary American government?

PART II — PRETEST

1. Procedure in the Supreme Court is surrounded by considerable ceremony. *All but one* of the following procedures is customary:
    a. The justices are always attired in their robes of office.
    b. Government attorneys wear morning clothes.
    c. All judges are seated in alphabetical order.
    d. Judges are introduced by the Clerk of the Court.

2. The chief basis for judicial decisions is probably
    a. precedent.
    b. public opinion.
    c. the party in power.
    d. checks and balances.

3. The judicial doctrine of *stare decisis* provides that the courts decide cases largely on the basis of
    a. present economic and social conditions.
    b. earlier court decisions.
    c. interpreting the will of Congress.
    d. equity.

4. Federal courts of appeal normally have
    a. original jurisdiction.
    b. grand juries.
    c. three-judge jury.
    d. judges with ten-year terms.

5. No decision can be rendered by the Supreme Court unless
    a. all nine judges participate.
    b. a quorum of five is present.
    c. six judges participate.
    d. at least two judges represent majority opinion.

6. At the Friday conference of Supreme Court justices, *all but one* of the following is true:
    a. The chief justice presides.
    b. The chief justice votes first.
    c. Each justice carries a red leather book.
    d. A majority decides the case.

7. The powers of the chief justice include *all but one* of the following:
    a. presiding over the Court
    b. choosing the opinion writer if justice has voted with the majority
    c. barring dissenting justices from the Friday conference
    d. leading conference discussion

8. The "rule of four" in Supreme Court procedure provides that four judges
    a. may adjourn the Court.
    b. grant a writ of *certiorari*.
    c. give priority to the order of hearing a case.
    d. are a quorum.

9. Critics of judicial activism believe that the courts should not try to make policy because
    a. judges are not elected.
    b. they do not represent all regions of the country.
    c. their terms do not coincide with that of the president.
    d. they do not have the necessary expertise.

10. After a grueling hearing that outraged women and liberal groups, the Senate Judiciary Committee narrowly confirmed
    a. Antonin Scalia.   c. Clarence Thomas.
    b. David Souter.   d. Sandra O'Connor.

11. Prayer in public schools
    a. cannot be on school property.
    b. is strictly unconstitutional.
    c. is constitutional if it is a nondenominational prayer.
    d. cannot be endorsed by school authorities.

12. What is the current standing of the Religious Freedom Restoration Act of 1993?
    a. upheld by the Court
    b. ruled unconstitutional by the Court
    c. Congress has ratified it every year since 1993.
    d. The status is still being decided by the Court.

13. The Amendment that is increasingly used to extend the Bill of Rights from national to state and local government is the
    a. Twenty-first.
    b. Eleventh.
    c. Twentieth.
    d. Fourteenth.

14. Newspapers claim that in addition to freedom to publish whatever they want, the First Amendment requires they also have
    a. freedom from subpoenas.
    b. freedom of confidentiality.
    c. freedom of access.
    d. all of the above

15. Governments may not censor what can be said, but they can regulate protests in all of the following ways *except*
    a. a requirement that all broadcast media devote at least 10 percent of airtime to political issues.
    b. requiring a limit on the number of protesters.
    c. requiring a reasonable location.
    d. a requirement to cover issues of public significance and reflect differing viewpoints.

PART III — PROGRAMMED PREVIEW

Knowledge Objective: To describe the differing forms of law on which the American legal system is based
1. Law based on judicial decisions of medieval English judges is _____ law.
2. Law based on judicial interpretation of the Constitution is _____ law.
3. A specific act of legislative body is _____ law.
4. Law based on exceptions from the common law in the interests of justice is _____ law.
5. The code of law emerging from bureaucratic decisions is _____ law.
6. The rule of precedent under which federal courts operate is called _____.
7. The concept that the courts should serve as a neutral referee between two contending parties is called the _____ system.

Knowledge Objective: To gain an overview of the organization of the federal court system
8. The lowest federal courts, in which nearly 700 judges preside, are _____ courts.
9. The federal courts that review district court decisions are courts of _____.
10. The highest federal court, with both original and appellate jurisdiction, is the _____.
11. The right to review cases already considered is _____.
12. The top U.S. prosecutor is the _____.

13. State and federal courts (do, do not) _____ exist in a superior-inferior relationship.
14. Much of the lower judicial work of the U.S. district is now carried out by _____.
15. Decisions of regulatory agencies can be reviewed by courts of _____.
16. Persons charged with a crime may get a reduced sentence by agreeing to a(n) _____.
17. The court officer who determines most appeals heard by the Supreme Court is the _____.

Knowledge Objective: *To study the major participants involved in selection of federal judges*
18. The custom that requires the president to consult with a state's senators before nominating a federal judge is called _____.
19. All potential nominees for federal judgeships are_____ by the American Bar Association.
20. In naming federal judges, the political affiliation of the nominee may be less important than the person's _____.
21. Presidential nominations to the Supreme Court are reviewed by the Senate _____.
22. In an attempt to avoid another Bork nomination battle, Bush nominated Souter, who had no _____ past record.
23. Bush's most controversial nomination to the Supreme Court was _____.
24. Congress controls the _____ and _____ of federal courts.

Knowledge Objective: *To discover how the Supreme Court operates*
25. The only cases heard by the Supreme Court are those selected by the _____.
26. Cases previously decided by lower courts are called up to the Supreme Court by writs of _____.
27. The normal upper time limit granted to counsel for each side in arguing a Supreme Court case is _____.
28. Supreme Court decisions are made in secret each week at the _____.
29. One use of published Supreme Court _____ is to communicate with the general public.

Knowledge Objective: *To evaluate the role of judicial review in a democratic society*
30. Over the past forty years more than 1,000 acts of _____ and _____ have been invalidated by the Supreme Court.
31. When the Supreme Court becomes greatly involved in political life, it is known as an _____ court.
32. Critics who believe that the Supreme Court has become too activist charge it with engaging in _____.
33. Chief Justice Rehnquist believes judges do pay attention to the great tides of _____.
34. The opponents of judicial activism believe that the Court should not become involved in _____ making.

PART IV — POST-TEST

1. An activist court, the critics say, is overly zealous in protecting the
   - a. poor.
   - b. property owners.
   - c. state officials.
   - d. military officers.

2. The federal court that has only original jurisdiction is
   - a. the Supreme Court.
   - b. district courts.
   - c. courts of appeal.
   - d. lower courts.

3. An adversary system of justice is one in which
   - a. the police bring charges.
   - b. the court is a neutral referee.
   - c. judges are political appointees.
   - d. justice is based on majority vote.

4. The top national official who has openly favored minority considerations in the judicial selection process has been
   - a. Carter.
   - b. Burger.
   - c. Ford.
   - d. Reagan.

5. The law that evolved from decisions interpreting our basic national governing document is
   - a. constitutional law.
   - b. administrative law.
   - c. equity law.
   - d. statutory law.

6. Several justices have timed their retirement to
   - a. ensure a replacement by a president sharing their views.
   - b. increase their retirement benefits.
   - c. bring fresh ideas to the Court.
   - d. avoid ruling on an issue where they have no competence.

7. Elections eventually influence Supreme Court decisions because
   - a. the judges try to do what the people want.
   - b. judges who are out of step are impeached.
   - c. new judges are appointed.
   - d. interest groups influence decisions.

8. In federal courts, justifiable disputes are
   - a. all constitutional questions.
   - b. those involving actual cases.
   - c. all administrative decisions.
   - d. those involving political questions.

9. The relationship between the state and federal court systems is
   - a. federal courts are always superior.
   - b. state courts have original jurisdiction.
   - c. they have interrelated responsibility.
   - d. they are completely separate.

10. If a Supreme Court justice agrees with the majority decision but differs on the reasoning, he files
    a. a concurring opinion.   c. articles of agreement.
    b. a dissenting opinion.   d. a minority opinion.

11. "Sunshine laws" generally apply to all *except*
    a. criminal trials.
    b. federal and state courtrooms.
    c. federal hearings as mandated by Congress.
    d. judicial conferences.

12. Which of the following has *not* been ruled unconstitutional in public schools?
    a. students praying in a school building
    b. recitation of the Lord's Prayer in an assembly
    c. posting of the Ten Commandments on the walls
    d. segregation based upon race

13. Which statement is *not* part of the so-called Lemon test?
    a. must avoid "excessive government entanglement with religion"
    b. A law must have a secular legislative purpose.
    c. It may inhibit religion.
    d. Christmas trees on public school property

14. The Bill of Rights was ratified
    a. by State legislatures prior to the signing of the Constitution.
    b. in the late 19th century.
    c. at the same time as the Constitution in 1787.
    d. in 1789 after the signing of the Constitution.

15. Which Supreme Court justice said of obscenity: "I know it when I see it"?
    a. Clarence Thomas
    b. Potter Stewart
    c. John Marshall Harlan
    d. Sandra Day O'Connor

PART V — TEST ANSWERS

Pretest

1.	c	6.	b	11.	d
2.	a	7.	c	12.	b
3.	b	8.	b	13.	d
4.	c	9.	a	14.	d
5.	c	10.	c	15.	d

Programmed Review

1. common
2. constitutional
3. statutory
4. equity
5. administrative
6. *stare decisis*
7. adversary
8. district
9. appeal
10. Supreme Court
11. appellate jurisdiction
12. attorney general
13. do not
14. magistrates
15. appeal
16. plea bargain
17. solicitor general
18. senatorial courtesy
19. evaluated
20. ideology
21. Judiciary Committee
22. visible
23. Clarence Thomas
24. structure; jurisdiction
25. Supreme Court
26. *certiorari*
27. thirty minutes
28. Friday conference
29. opinion
30. legislatures; city councils
31. activist
32. judicial legislation
33. public opinion
34. policy

Post-test

1.	a	6.	a	11.	d
2.	b	7.	c	12.	a
3.	b	8.	b	13.	c
4.	a	9.	c	14.	d
5.	a	10.	a	15.	b

Chapter 15
First Amendment Freedoms

PART I — LEARNING OBJECTIVES

15.1   What did the framers hope to achieve by spelling out the basic rights of American citizens?

15.2   Why did the framers of the Constitution believe a Bill of Rights was necessary?

15.3   Which two clauses in the Constitution deal with freedom of religion?

15.4   What does the Constitution guarantee in regard to religion?

15.5   What kinds of speech are protected under the Constitution?

15.6   How has the definition of protected speech changed over the course of American history?

15.7   What kinds of speech are not protected under the Constitution?

15.8   Why aren't some forms of speech protected under the Constitution?

15.9   Why is a free press so important to the maintenance of democracy?

15.10   Are there limits on the freedom of the press?

15.11   If there are limits on the freedom of the press, what are these limits?

15.12   What is the relationship between the freedom of assembly and petition and American forms of political organization and behavior?

PART II — PRETEST

1. Specifically, the Bill of Rights ratified in 1791 was aimed at
    a. the national government.
    b. the state governments.
    c. both national and state government.
    d. providing unlimited freedom to the people.

2. The due process clause, interpreted to mean that the states could not abridge the First Amendment freedoms, is part of the
    a. Fifteenth Amendment.   c. Eighteenth Amendment.
    b. Fourteenth Amendment.   d. Thirteenth Amendment.

3. Because of the establishment clause, states may not
    a. teach the Darwinian theory of evolution.
    b. study the Bible or religion in public schools.
    c. permit religious instructors to teach in public schools during the day.
    d. establish Blue Laws.

4. The Supreme Court has held that tax funds may not be used to
    a. provide sign-language interpretation for deaf parochial school students.
    b. furnish guidance and remedial help in parochial schools.
    c. pay fares to send children to church-operated schools.
    d. pay parochial teachers' salaries.

5. The doctrine that free speech cannot be restricted unless there is a close connection between a speech and illegal action is called
    a. the clear and present danger test.
    b. the speech and dangerous result test.
    c. the speech and action test.
    d absolutist doctrine.

6. Of all forms of government interference with expression, judges are most suspicious of those that
    a. trespass on First Amendment freedoms.
    b. limit freedom of speech of any kind.
    c. impose prior restraints on publication.
    d. impose *a posteriori* restraints.

7. The current standards for obscenity are made
    a. by the Supreme Court.
    b. at the state level.
    c. at the community level.
    d. by Congress.

8. Persons may be convicted for one of the following:
    a. possessing obscene materials
    b. selling obscene literature
    c. importing obscene literature from abroad
    d. writing obscene material

9. Street marches by protest groups are protected by the First Amendment right to
    a. assemble.
    b. petition.
    c. demonstrate.
    d. boycott.

10. All of the following are forms of nonprotected speech *except*
    a. libel.
    b. symbolic speech.
    c. obscenity.
    d. commercial speech.

11. To be subject to sanctions, "fighting words" must
    a. create anger, alarm, or resentment.
    b. incite acts of violence.
    c. be based on gender.
    d. be based on race, ethnicity, or religion.

12. The _____ clause has been interpreted by the Supreme Court to forbid governmental support to any or all religions.
    a. supremacy
    b. establishment
    c. exercise
    d. due process

13. Prayer in public schools
    a. is strictly unconstitutional.
    b. is constitutional if it is a nondenominational prayer.
    c. cannot be on school property.
    d. cannot be endorsed by school authorities.

14. "Libel" is
    a. generally applied in cases where private citizens criticize public officials.
    b. written defamation of another person.
    c. subject to tests of truth.
    d. spoken defamation of character.

15. The FCC fined Infinity Broadcasting for indecent remarks made by
    a. Howard Stern.
    b. Khallid Abdul Muhammad.
    c. Jim Hightower.
    d. Michael Moore

PART III — PROGRAMMED REVIEW

Knowledge Objective: To examine constitutional safeguards of freedom
1. The first ten amendments to the Constitution are known as _____.
2. The nationalization of the Bill of Rights was an _____ process whereby the Supreme Court selectively applied them to state and local governments via the due process clause.
3. The _____ clause of the Fourteenth Amendment protects freedom of the press and of speech from impairment by the states.
4. *Gitlow v. New York* (1925) extended the _____ Amendment rights via the Fourteenth Amendment.

Knowledge Objective: To inquire into the meaning of the wall of separation between church and state
5. The _____ clause is designed to prevent three main evils: sponsorship, financial support, and active involvement of the government in religious activity.
6. The _____ restored use of the compelling interest test.
7. The Supreme Court has held that a publicly sponsored Nativity scene (is, is not) _____ constitutional if the basic purpose is commercial.

8. Because of the establishment clause, states may not prohibit the teaching of Darwin's theory of evolution or require the simultaneous teaching of _____.

9. The Supreme Court has ruled that tax funds (may, may not) _____ be used for lunches, transportation, and remedial assistance in religious primary and secondary schools.

10. Sponsorship of prayer in school buildings by public school authorities (is, is not) _____ constitutional.

11. The Supreme Court (has, has not) _____ upheld the right of parents to deduct from their state taxes expenses incurred in sending children to public or private schools.

Knowledge Objective: To analyze the relationship between free speech and a free people

12. Government's constitutional power to regulate speech involves three forms: beliefs, speech, and _____.

13. The limits of free speech were set forth as the _____ test by Justice Holmes in *Schenck v. United States*.

14. The _____ position doctrine takes the view that freedom of expression has the highest priority.

15. Of all forms of governmental interference with expression, judges are most suspicious of those that impose _____ restraint on publication.

16. When people of common intelligence differ on the requirements of a law, it is unconstitutional on the grounds of _____.

Knowledge Objective: To investigate the scope of freedom of the press

17. In a recent decision the Supreme Court (did, did not) _____ support barring of the press from a criminal case.

18. In 1996, Congress made it a federal crime to use the _____ to knowingly transmit indecent material to minors.

19. More than ____ percent of requests under the FOIA have been granted.

20. Censorship of the mails is _____.

21. The _____ acts make most nonclassified records of federal agencies public.

22. Many states have passed_____ laws requiring most government agencies to open their meetings to the public and the press.

23. Household censorship is (constitutional, unconstitutional)_____.

24. The federal regulation of radio and television is based on the _____ of broadcast channels available.

25. Current federal laws (do, do not)_____ protect commercial speech.

Knowledge Objective: To define limits on speech (libel, obscenity) that are constitutional

26. The First Amendment (does, does not) _____ prevent the FCC from refusing to renew a radio license if in its opinion a broadcaster has not served the public interest.

27. The _____ doctrine concerns censorship before a speech is made.
28. The mere fact that a statement is wrong or even defamatory is not sufficient to sustain a charge of _____.
29. Under the current test a jury determines whether or not a work appeals to prurient interests or is patently offensive to _____ standards.
30. Obscenity (is, is not) _____ entitled to constitutional protection.
31. Pornographic books and x-rated movies are entitled to (less, the same) _____ protection than political speech.
32. Cities may regulate by _____ where adult motion picture theaters may be located.
33. Sexually explicit materials either about minors or aimed at them (are, are not) _____ prohibited by the First Amendment.

Knowledge Objective: To examine the right of the people peaceably to assemble and to petition the government
34. The right to assemble peaceably applies not only to meetings in private homes, but to gatherings held in _____.
35. The right to assemble and to petition does not include the right to _____ on private property.
36. The right of the Million Youth Rally to march on the streets (has, has not) _____ been upheld by the courts.
37. In the late eighteenth century the _____ Act made it a crime to utter false, scandalous, or malicious statements intended to bring the government or any of its officers into disrepute.
38. In general, peaceful civil disobedience (is, is not) _____ a protected right.
39. Seditious speech (is, is not) _____ protected when it advocates violence.
40. Privately owned shopping malls are neither public _____ nor places of public _____.

PART IV — POST-TEST

1. What types of governmental meetings are not open to the public?
   a. judicial conferences
   b. federal trials
   c. congressional committee meetings
   d. local school board meetings

2. The bad tendency doctrine gives to _____ the power to decide what kinds of speech can be outlawed.
   a. courts
   b. legislatures
   c. the people
   d. chief executives

3. Constitutional restrictions on establishment of religion include
    a. persons praying in school buildings.
    b. classes observing a moment of silence.
    c. public officials sponsoring nondenominational prayer at primary and secondary school graduations.
    d. studying the Bible.

4. The Freedom of Information Act of 1966 concerns
    a. censorship.
    b. press responsibility and fairness.
    c. abuses in the overclassification of documents.
    d. the right to privacy.

5. The Telecommunications Act of 1996 provided for *all but one* of the following:
    a. competition among telephone companies and cable TV
    b. requirement of v-chips in new television sets
    c. elimination of government regulation of the airways
    d. Communications Decency Act

6. In *Miller v. California* (1973), Chief Justice Burger defined obscenity as a work that
    a. lacks serious artistic, political, or scientific value.
    b. does not apply traditional standards of morality.
    c. is utterly without redeeming value.
    d. graphically describes sexual activity.

7. The distribution of religious and political pamphlets, leaflets, and handbills to the public is
    a. constitutionally protected.
    b. under almost all circumstances locally prosecuted.
    c. constitutionally ignored.
    d. prohibited without a license.

8. Of the following, which has the greatest restrictions placed upon it by the Constitution?
    a. speech
    b. assembly
    c. picketing
    d. petitions

9. Persons may have no constitutional right to engage in political action in
    a. any area designed to serve purposes other than demonstrations.
    b. courthouses.
    c. schools.
    d. privately owned shopping malls.

10. "Shield laws" pertain to freedom of
    a. assembly.
    b. the press.
    c. motion picture producers.
    d. Internet use.

11. "Sunshine laws" generally apply to all *except*
    a. judicial conferences.
    b. federal and state courtrooms.
    c. federal hearings as mandated by Congress.
    d. criminal trials.

12. The most controversial freedom associated with expression is that of
    a. speech.
    b. actions.
    c. belief.
    d. peaceful assembly.

13. In 2002, from where did most immigrants to the United States come?
    a. Europe
    b. Africa
    c. North America
    d. South America

14. The nonpreferentialist test
    a. precludes favoritism toward a particular religion.
    b. does not preclude government accommodation of some religious activities.
    c. does not prevent government support for some religious activities.
    d. all of the above

15. "Prior restraint" is constitutional when
    a. school authorities exercise editorial control over the style and content of student speech in high school newspapers.
    b. related to some military and security matters.
    c. both a and b
    d. neither a nor b

PART V — TEST ANSWERS

Pretest

1. a	6. c	11. b
2. b	7. c	12. b
3. c	8. c	13. d
4. d	9. a	14. b
5. a	10. b	15. a

Programmed Review

1. Bill of Rights
2. evolutionary
3. due process
4. First
5. establishment
6. Restoration of Religious Freedom Act of 1993
7. is
8. creation science
9. may
10. is not
11. has
12. action
13. clear and present danger
14. preferred
15. prior
16. vagueness
17. did not
18. Internet
19. 90
20. unconstitutional
21. Freedom of Information
22. sunshine
23. constitutional
24. scarcity
25. do not
26. does not
27. prior restraint
28. libel
29. community
30. is not
31. less
32. zoning
33. are
34. public streets
35. trespass
36. has
37. Sedition
38. is not
39. is not
40. streets; assembly

Post-test

1. a	6. a	11. a
2. b	7. a	12. a
3. c	8. c	13. c
4. c	9. d	14. d
5. c	10. b	15. c

Chapter 16
Rights to Life, Liberty, and Property

PART I — LEARNING OBJECTIVES

16.1   What arguments have been made for and against a constitutional right to privacy?
16.2   What kinds of behavior are covered by a constitutional right to privacy?
16.3   What rights do the accused have in an American court of law?
16.4   How is U.S. citizenship acquired and retained?
16.5   In what ways does the Constitution protect the property rights of U.S. citizens?
16.6   What powers and responsibilities are associated with U.S. citizenship?
16.7   Why are there limitations on the practical ability of the Supreme Court to define the meaning of the Bill of Rights?

PART II — PRETEST

1. Rules and regulations that restrain those in government who exercise power are referred to as
   a. police powers.
   b. expatriation rights.
   c. immunity rights.
   d. due process.

2. Current immigration law
   a. allows legally admitted aliens to be deported if they commit crimes.
   b. is based on the prefrerential norm of "family reunification."
   c. does permit political refugees to be admitted.
   d. prevents legally admitted aliens from being deported under any circumstances.

3. All of the following are exceptions to the general rule against warrantless searches/seizures *except*
   a. the plain-view exception.
   b. exigent circumstances.
   c. the "automobile" exception.
   d. the "residence" exception.

4. Persons who are arrested by federal officers at the scene of a crime are presumed to be
   a. guilty.
   b. innocent.
   c. accomplices.
   d. suspect.

5. Federally guaranteed rights include all of the following *except*
   a. no double jeopardy.
   b. right to counsel.
   c. excessive fines and unusual punishments.
   d. parole and/or probation.

6. The concept that private property cannot be taken for public use without just compensation is
   a. eminent domain.
   b. habeas corpus.
   c. *ex post facto* law.
   d. martial law.

7. Protection against self-incrimination should prevent
   a. double jeopardy.
   b. habeas corpus.
   c. eminent domain.
   d. police brutality.

8. Aliens do not have the right to
   a. jury trial.
   b. freedom of religion.
   c. vote.
   d. attend school.

9. A true bill or indictment is associated with
   a. a petit jury.
   b. plea bargaining.
   c. eminent domain.
   d. a grand jury.

10. Substantive due process today is primarily concerned with
    a. property rights.
    b. social policy.
    c. civil liberties.
    d. economic regulation.

11. Who has the unrestricted right to live and travel in the United States?
    a. American citizens
    b. registered aliens
    c. any person except citizens of North Korea and Cuba
    d. the children of political prisoners throughout the world

12. An "impartial jury" must
    a. consist of persons who represent a fair cross-section of the community.
    b. be appointed by the prosecution.
    c. consist of people that have a high school education.
    d. be experts to consider testimony.

13. The right to renounce citizenship is called
    a. renunciation.
    b. expatriation.
    c. abdication.
    d. naturalization.

14. Which of the following is *not* guaranteed to all persons in the United States?
    a. freedom to be employed at any job
    b. freedom of religion
    c. freedom of speech
    d. freedom of press

15. In the decision concerning *Griswold v. Connecticut* (1965), the Supreme Court relied on
    a. principles relating to procedural due process.
    b. the right to privacy as implied in the First, Third, Fourth, Fifth, Ninth, and Fourteenth Amendments.
    c. specific references to "right to life" as implied in the First, Fourth, Fifth, Ninth, and Fourteenth Amendments.
    d. the moral suasion of the general public.

PART III — PROGRAMMED REVIEW

Knowledge Objective: To review our constitutional rights to life, liberty, and property
1. _____ is the established rules and regulations that restrain those in government who exercise power.
2. _____ is the legal action conferring citizenship upon an alien.
3. An applicant for naturalization must be _____ years of age.

Knowledge Objective: To analyze how the Constitution protects citizenship
4. Citizenship was given constitutional protection in 1868 with the adoption of the _____ Amendment.
5. Dual citizenship for Americans grows by _____ per year.
6. The right of individuals to renounce their citizenship is the _____ of _____.
7. The immigration law of 1986 attempted to deal with _____ aliens.
8. There are currently _____ to _____ million undocumented aliens (estimated).
9. Millions of illegal aliens have entered the United States from _____.

Knowledge Objective: To examine constitutional protections of property
10. _____ v. _____ laid the basis for the landmark *Roe v. Wade* case.
11. The due process of law clause is contained in both the _____ and _____ Amendments.
12. There are two kinds of due process, _____ and _____.
13. Procedural due process (does, does not) _____ apply to many methods of law enforcement.
14. The unrestricted right of women to have an abortion during the first trimester of pregnancy is an example of _____ due process.
15. The Supreme Court (has, has not) _____ ruled that state employees are entitled to due process hearings before being fired.
16. A stop and frisk exception to searches (was, was not) _____ upheld by the Supreme Court in 1968.

17. State laws that prohibit homosexual acts in private homes have been (upheld, struck down) _____ by the Supreme Court.
18. _____ due process places limits on how governmental power may be exercised.
19. _____ due process places limits on why governmental power may be exercised.
20. Substantive due process deals with the _____ of the law.

Knowledge Objective: To inquire into arbitrary arrest, questioning, and imprisonment
21. Officers (may, may not) _____ stop and search suspects if they have reason to believe they are armed and dangerous.
22. A search warrant must describe what places are to be _____ and the things that are to be _____.
23. In *Mapp v. Ohio,* the Supreme Court ruled that evidence obtained unconstitutionally (can, cannot) _____ be used in a criminal trial.
24. Witnesses before a congressional committee may not refuse to testify if they have been granted _____.
25. Critics of the exclusionary rule argue that the solution is to punish the (police, suspect) _____.
26. In *Miranda v. Arizona,* the Supreme Court held that a conviction (could, could not) _____ stand if evidence introduced at the trial was a result of "custodial interrogation."
27. President Bush declared that foreign terrorists were to be classified as enemy _____.
28. Double jeopardy prevents two criminal trials by the _____ government for the same _____ offense.

Knowledge Objective: To evaluate our system of justice
29. Critics who claim our justice system is unreliable often point to trial by _____ as the chief source of trouble.
30. The targeting of racial minorities as potential suspects is called _____.
31. Many members of minorities (do, do not)_____ think that they have equal protection under the law.
32. In the United States, our emphasis on judicial protection of civil liberties focuses attention on the _____.
33. In the 1990s states have chosen to re-write jury system laws to counter the effects of _____.
34. Programs to move police from patrol cars into neighborhoods and to work with groups in society is called _____.
35. Double jeopardy protections may not prevent a defendant from being subjected to both _____ and _____ trials.

PART IV — POST-TEST

1. To become a citizen of the United States, aliens have to do all of the following things *except*
    a. renounce allegiance to their native country.
    b. swear that they will bear arms for the U.S.
    c. swear to defend the Constitution.
    d. own property worth at least $2,000.

2. Naturalized citizens are not required to demonstrate that they
    a. are of good moral character.
    b. are able to speak and write English.
    c. know the principles of U.S. government.
    d. have a sponsoring family.

3. In its efforts to block the entry of illegal aliens, the Naturalization Service has been
    a. moderately successful.   c. extremely successful.
    b. unsuccessful.   d. uninvolved.

4. Under *Roe v. Wade* the Court held that a woman in her first three months of pregnancy had a(n) _____ right to abortion.
    a. no   c. court approved
    b. limited   d. unrestricted

5. In 2003, the U.S. Supreme Court struck down a _____ state law making homosexual sodomy a crime.
    a. Georgia   c. California
    b. Massachusetts   d. Texas

6. A criminal who pleads guilty to an offense that is lesser than the one with which he had been charged is said to have engaged in
    a. the exclusionary process.   c. plea bargaining.
    b. self-incrimination.   d. double jeopardy.

7. What element(s) must be present for the "exclusionary rule," which provides that certain evidence cannot be used to convict a person in a criminal trial, to be applicable?
    a. employees against employers
    b. children against parents
    c. illegal police searches
    d. testimony given in exchange for immunity

8. As a result of the *Miranda* decision, all persons accused of a crime have the following rights except
   a. to remain silent.
   b. have a lawyer represent them.
   c. freedom on bail.
   d. halt their interrogation any point.

9. In the 1990s, the Rehnquist Court made it easier to do all of the following *except*
   a. cut back on appeals.
   b. impose death sentences.
   c. carry out executions.
   d. appeal a plea bargain.

10. In the last decade, the number of death row inmates has
   a. increased slightly.
   b. decreased slightly.
   c. increased dramatically.
   d. decreased dramatically.

11. Procedural due process refers to the
   a. appropriate procedures for writing laws.
   b. idea that unreasonable laws are unconstitutional.
   c. methods by which a law is applied.
   d. limitations on what a government may do.

12. The Supreme Court, in _____, struck down a Colorado initiative that prohibited state and local government from protecting homosexuals from discrimination.
   a. *Lawrence v. Texas*
   b. *Roe v. Wade*
   c. *Romer v. Evans*
   d. *Clinton v. New York*

13. "Due process" clauses are found in
   a. the Fifth and Fourteenth Amendments.
   b. Article II of the Constitution and the Fifth Amendment.
   c. the Fourteenth Amendment.
   d. the Fifth Amendment.

14. A constitutional requirement that government act reasonably and laws be fair and reasonable is called
   a. substantive due process.
   b. procedural due process.
   c. definitive due process.
   d. judicial due process.

15. Individuals requesting political asylum must show
    a. individual danger of persecution.
    b. fears of persecution based on religion, race, nationality, or membership in a particular social group.
    c. that they escaped terrible conditions.
    d. that they cannot return home without fear of retribution.

PART V — TEST ANSWERS

Pretest

1.	d	6.	a	11.	a
2.	a	7.	d	12.	a
3.	d	8.	c	13.	b
4.	b	9.	d	14.	a
5.	c	10.	c	15.	b

Programmed Review

1. Due process
2. Naturalization
3. over 18
4. Fourteenth
5. 50,000
6. right of expatriation
7. undocumented
8. 2.3; 2.4
9. Mexico
10. *Griswold v. Connecticut*
11. Fifth; Fourteenth
12. procedural; substantive
13. does
14. substantive
15. has
16. was
17. upheld
18. Procedural
19. Substantive
20. content
21. may
22. searched; seized
23. cannot
24. immunity
25. police
26. could not
27. combatants
28. same; criminal
29. jury
30. racial profiling
31. do not
32. Supreme Court
33. nullification
34. community policing
35. civil; criminal

Post-test

1.	d	6.	c	11.	c
2.	d	7.	c	12.	c
3.	b	8.	c	13.	a
4.	d	9.	d	14.	a
5.	d	10.	c	15.	a

Chapter 17
Equal Rights under the Law

PART I — LEARNING OBJECTIVES

17.1   What do we mean by "equality" in the context of American society, law, and politics?

17.2   What are the historical roots of contemporary notions of equality?

17.3   What is meant by the phrase "equal protection of the law"?

17.4   What groups and forces contributed to the expansion of civil rights in America?

17.5   What are the most important civil rights issues facing America today?

17.6   What is meant by "affirmative action"?

17.7   What are the most important arguments for and against affirmative action programs?

PART II — PRETEST

1. Since 1960 the women's movement has not concentrated on
   - a. pay.
   - b. pensions.
   - c. parenthood.
   - d. peace.

2. The "boat people" refugees applied to which minority group?
   - a. Chicanos
   - b. Puerto Ricans
   - c. Asian Americans
   - d. African Americans

3. The civil rights gains of the 1960s chiefly benefited
   - a. young black males.
   - b. black welfare mothers.
   - c. the black middle class.
   - d. poverty stricken blacks.

4. Half of all Hispanic Americans live in the two U.S. states of
   - a. California and Texas.
   - b. Florida and New Mexico.
   - c. New York and Louisiana.
   - d. Michigan and Arizona.

5. A state legislature may classify people only if the classification meets a _____ test.
   - a. suspect
   - b. almost suspect
   - c. fundamental rights
   - d. rational basis

6. The 1896 Supreme Court ruling that approved of "separate but equal" was
   - a. *Brown v. Board of Education.*
   - b. *Roe v. Wade.*
   - c. *Plessy v. Ferguson.*
   - d. *Dred Scott.*

7. One of the following is unconstitutional as an age classification.
   a. Driver licenses may not be issued to those under 16.
   b. Alcohol may not be sold to those persons under 21.
   c. A state policeman is retired at age 55.
   d. An applicant for a teaching position (age 57) is rejected on the basis of age.

8. Slavery was abolished and African Americans' equal rights were granted by the _____ Amendments.
   a. Eighteenth, Nineteenth, and Twentieth
   b. Thirteenth, Fourteenth, and Fifteenth
   c. Sixteenth, Seventeenth, and Eighteenth
   d. Twelfth and Sixteenth

9. In the 1930s, African Americans resorted to which of these strategies to secure their rights?
   a. violence
   b. political power
   c. litigation
   d. persuasion

10. The civil rights movement produced its first charismatic leader during the Montgomery, Alabama, bus boycott of 1955.
    a. James Baldwin
    b. Dick Gregory
    c. Martin Luther King Jr.
    d. Jesse Jackson

11. Legislation designed and enacted in 1965 that was to ensure that no person would be deprived of the right to vote in any election for any office because of color or race was the
    a. Civil Rights Act.
    b. Voting Registration Act.
    c. Voting Rights Act.
    d. Election Reform Laws.

12. An example of a quasi-suspect class that requires heightened scrutiny is
    a. gender.
    b. age.
    c. disability.
    d. race.

13. Under Title VII of the Civil Rights Act, age, sex, and handicap may
    a. be considered where occupational qualifications are absolutely necessary to the normal operation of a particular business.
    b. be considered when it involves veteran disabilities.
    c. not be considered when hiring or in promotions.
    d. be considered by private employers.

14. Private individuals may discriminate if they
    a. do not indicate any preference in their advertising.
    b. rent houses without the service of an agent.
    c. own no more than three houses or have no more than four separate living units.
    d. all of the above

15. A(n) _____ is a tract of land given to the Native American tribal nations by treaty.
    a. allotment
    b. reservation
    c. preserve
    d. forest preserve

PART III — PROGRAMMED REVIEW

Knowledge Objective: To examine the role of government in providing equal rights
1. Most Americans do not accept the equality of (opportunity, results) _____.
2. Affirmative action is designed to help people disadvantaged by their _____ memberships.
3. The focus of the modern women's rights movement has been to secure adoption of the _____ Amendment.
4. A major handicap of the Hispanics has been their _____, which is not mainstream America.
5. Hispanics were courted by both presidential candidates in the year _____.
6. A 1988 law provided $20,000 as restitution to _____ interned during World War II.
7. Native Americans are a separate people with power to regulate their own internal affairs, subject to _____ supervision.
8. After the Civil War, three "civil rights" amendments were added to the Constitution, the _____, _____ and _____ Amendments.
9. The first branch of the national government to become sensitized to the aspirations of African Americans was the _____.
10. In the 1930s, blacks resorted to _____ to secure their rights.
11. In the 1960s, the use of litigation by blacks was supplemented by a widespread _____, _____ and _____ movement.
12. The immediate origin of the black revolt occurred in 1955 when a _____ boycott was organized in Montgomery, Alabama.
13. A U.S. Civil Rights commission found that Asian Americans (do, do not) _____ face widespread discrimination.

Knowledge Objective: To examine equal protection under the laws
14. The equal protection of the laws clause is part of the _____ Amendment and is implied in the due process clause of the _____ Amendment.
15. The Constitution forbids only _____ classification.
16. The traditional test of whether a law complies with the equal protection requirement is the _____ basis test.

17. Race and national origins are obviously _____ classifications.
18. The quasi-suspect classification includes _____ and _____.
19. More than a generation after the Kerner Report, life for inner-city minorities is _____.
20. Poverty, according to the Supreme Court, (is, is not) _____ an unconstitutional classification.
21. Age (can, cannot) _____ be used as a criterion in employment if it is related to proper job performance.

Knowledge Objective: To describe the life and death of Jim Crow in education
22. In the 1954 case of _____ v. _____ the Supreme Court reversed its 1896 decision in *Plessy v. Ferguson.*
23. Segregation required by law is called _____ segregation.
24. When segregation occurs without sanction of law, it is called _____ segregation.
25. Busing across school district lines (is, is not) _____ required if the school district lines have been drawn to maintain segregation.

Knowledge Objective: To review barriers to voting
26. Most suffrage requirements, inside the U.S. constitutional framework, are fixed by the _____.
27. The Voting Rights Act of 1965 has been (effective, ineffective) _____.
28. The poll tax was abolished in federal elections by the _____ Amendment.
29. The Voting Rights Act of 1965 as amended set aside _____ tests throughout the country.
30. In attempting to give minorities a majority district, the result will probably be more minority districts and more safe _____ districts.
31. In _____ v. _____ the Supreme Court ruled that race cannot be the sole reason for drawing voting district lines.

Knowledge Objective: To examine racial and sexual barriers to public accommodations, jobs, and homes
32. The Fourteenth Amendment applies only to _____ action and not to private groups serving only their own members.
33. Segregation in places of _____ accommodation is unconstitutional.
34. A training program that gives preference to minorities or women (is, is not) _____ constitutional.
35. The Court (upheld, struck down) _____ the Richmond, Virginia, plan to require nonminority contractors to subcontract work to minority business.
36. Attempts through legislation to end housing discrimination (have, have not) _____ been a great success.
37. In the *Bakke* case the Supreme Court held that a special admissions category from which whites were excluded was (constitutional, unconstitutional) _____.
38. To redress the discrimination suffered by minorities, governments have adopted _____ programs.

39. Affirmative action programs may temporarily set _____ but not _____.
40. The adoption of California's Proposition 209 outlawed _____ programs.

PART IV — POST-TEST

1. Upon passage of the Nineteenth Amendment, women
    a. received equal pay.
    b. received equal rights.
    c. put an end to legal discrimination.
    d. got the right to vote.

2. Identify the unrelated word.
    a. freedom rides
    b. sit-ins
    c. bus boycott
    d. violence

3. The Kerner Report declared that
    a. violence is as American as apple pie.
    b. our nation was moving toward two societies, separate and unequal.
    c. affirmative action is un-American.
    d. black children should have neighborhood schools.

4. The minority with the greatest voting potential is
    a. Indians.
    b. Vietnamese.
    c. Hispanics.
    d. African Americans.

5. A reasonable government classification would be based on
    a. age.
    b. religion.
    c. sex.
    d. race.

6. Since 1960 the national government's role in the issue of equal rights has been to
    a. support discrimination.
    b. remain neutral.
    c. take affirmative action.
    d. defer to the states.

7. One of the following situations is outside government jurisdiction.
    a. a restaurant bars men without jacket and tie
    b. a hotel refuses to register a rock-and-roll star
    c. a realtor refuses to sell property to an extended Vietnamese family
    d. a theater refuses to seat a group with long hair and blue jeans

8. _____ is a fundamental right.
    a. Travel
    b. Housing
    c. Welfare
    d. Education

9. Which of these cases marked the end of the separate but equal interpretation of the Constitution?
    a. *Plessy v. Ferguson*
    b. *Weber v. Kaiser*
    c. *Bakke v. California Regents*
    d. *Brown v. Board of Education*

10. The 2003 case, _____, reaffirmed *Bakke* on the permissibility of affirmative action programs.
    a. *Brown v. Board of Education*
    b. *Grutter v. Bollinger*
    c. *Richmond v. Croson*
    d. *Boy Scouts of America v. Dale*

11. The fact that a law has a differential effect, or disparate impact, on persons of differing race or sex
    a. is not important.
    b. cannot be used as evidence in a court of law.
    c. establishes the fact that the law is unconstitutional.
    d. does not establish the fact that the law is unconstitutional.

12. The Supreme Court asserts that veterans' preferences are
    a. constitutional because veterans are not a suspect class.
    b. constitutional even if they do keep women from getting jobs.
    c. unconstitutional because veterans are a suspect class.
    d. unconstitutional because they keep women from getting jobs.

13. With regard to the drawing and redistricting of voting areas, states
    a. may make up for past discriminatory gerrymandering by temporary redistricting.
    b. may not redistrict but must return to historically defined voting areas.
    c. may make race the sole reason for drawing district lines when it will ensure that a minority group will have minority group representation.
    d. may not make race the sole reason for drawing district lines.

14. The California Proposition that denied medical, educational, and social services to illegal immigrants was
    a. Proposition 11.
    b. Proposition 13.
    c. Proposition 200.
    d. Proposition 187.

15. Nearly one-third of Filipino Americans live in
    a. Texas.
    b. New York.
    c. Florida.
    d. California.

PART V — TEST ANSWERS

Pretest

1. c	6. c	11. c
2. c	7. d	12. a
3. d	8. b	13. a
4. a	9. c	14. d
5. d	10. c	15. b

Programmed Review

1. results
2. group
3. Equal Rights
4. language
5. 2000
6. Japanese-Americans
7. congressional
8. Thirteenth; Fourteenth; Fifteenth
9. executive
10. litigation
11. social; economic; political
12. bus
13. do
14. Fourteenth; Fifth
15. unreasonable
16. rational
17. suspect
18. sex; illegitimacy
19. worse
20. is not
21. can
22. *Brown v. Board of Education*
23. de jure
24. de facto
25. is
26. states
27. effective
28. Twenty-fourth
29. literacy
30. Republican
31. *Shaw v. Reno*
32. government
33. public
34. is
35. struck down
36. have not
37. unconstitutional
38. affirmative action
39. goals; quotas
40. affirmative action

Post-test

1. d	6. c	11. d
2. d	7. a	12. b
3. b	8. a	13. d
4. c	9. d	14. d
5. a	10. b	15. d

Epilogue
Sustaining Constitutional Democracy

PART I — LEARNING OBJECTIVES

18.1 Describe how the Constitution established a restrained and responsive government.

18.2 Compare the qualities of representative and participatory democracies.

18.3 Explain two basic ways of organizing representation.

18.4 Describe broker rule and its relationship to fair representation.

18.5 Explain reasons for the gap between public conceptions of the ideal and the actual politician.

18.6 Discuss the situational and contextual aspects of leadership.

18.7 Explain the difference between leaders and managers.

18.8 Describe the qualities needed for good leadership.

18.9 Discuss why opposing ideas and an organized opposition are necessary to democracy.

18.10 Assess the connections between an informed and educated citizenry and democratic government.

PART II — PRETEST

1. The "ultimate test" of a democratic system is the legal existence of a
   - a. competitive party system.
   - b. free educational system.
   - c. free market.
   - d. recognized opposition.

2. American politicians tend to win their great acclaim
   - a. shortly after election.
   - b. while running for office.
   - c. after death.
   - d. when they win reelection.

3. Critics of broker rule believe all of the following *except*
   - a. election laws are too complicated.
   - b. low-income persons are less heard.
   - c. parties do not offer meaningful alternatives.
   - d. a bias exists for the status quo.

4. At the very heart of those personal characteristics that motivate politicians is
   a. ideology.
   b. ambition.
   c. selfishness.
   d. craftiness.

5. A Greek spokesman who declared that government was everyone's business is
   a. Socrates.
   b. Pericles.
   c. Zorba.
   d. Heroditus.

6. The most important element in American government today is
   a. interest groups.
   b. committed citizens.
   c. great leaders.
   d. obedient followers.

7. Direct participation in decision making
   a. will enhance the dignity of the individuals involved.
   b. will act as a safeguard against dictatorship.
   c. rests on a theory of self-protection.
   d. all of the above

8. Direct democracy works best when
   a. an area is small.
   b. a society is pluralistic.
   c. people are well educated.
   d. standards of living are high.

9. Participatory democracy works best in
   a. neighborhood associations.
   b. cities.
   c. states.
   d. the armed forces.

10. Broker rule is best described as
    a. compromises between conflicting groups.
    b. substituting interest groups for parties.
    c. regulation by the New York Stock Exchange.
    d. giving women greater power.

11. The best representation of minorities is likely within
    a. reserved seats in legislatures.
    b. direct democracy.
    c. affirmative action programs in the administrative side of government.
    d. broker rule.

12. The framers of the Constitution valued above all the principle of
    a. individual liberty.
    b. the right of dissent.
    c. property rights.
    d. justice.

13. Indispensable qualities of leadership include
    a. self-confidence.
    b. humility.
    c. realism.
    d. patience.

14. What did the framers of the Constitution believe to be the cause of the decline of ancient Athens?
    a. freedom
    b. security
    c. lack of responsibility
    d. all of the above

15. The ultimate test of a democratic system is the legal existence of a(n)
    a. written constitution.
    b. system of checks and balances.
    c. provision for separation of powers.
    d. officially recognized opposition.

PART III — PROGRAMMED REVIEW

Knowledge Objective: To analyze the democratic faith
1. According to democratic theory, the only legitimate foundation for any government is the _____ of the people.
2. The democratic concept in practice is a mixture of _____ and _____.
3. In the full span of human history, most people have lived under _____ rule.
4. Freedom and _____ go together.
5. As Athens declined, Athenians wanted _____ more than liberty or freedom.
6. Leadership is important in a democracy, but even more important is an _____ citizenry.
7. The American community came together after the _____ attacks of 9/11.

Knowledge Objective: To review the basic guiding principles of American democratic government
8. _____ was the principle most valued by the framers.
9. The Constitution both _____ and _____ power to national, state, and local governments.
10. The Constitution distributes power between the _____ and _____ governments.
11. Efficiency (was, was not) _____ the main goal of the framers.
12. The framers tried to protect individual liberty _____ government.
13. The framers wanted to make government responsive to the people but to insulate it from momentary _____.

Knowledge Objective: To examine the prospects for American democratic government
14. Individual needs and the needs of society must be _____.
15. Negotiations between interest groups within the Congress that result in compromise legislation is called _____ rule.
16. Democratic governments always have _____ groups that are free to speak out.

Knowledge Objective: To analyze American attitudes toward politicians
17. American citizens (are, are not) _____ normally critical of their government.
18. Leadership can be understood only in the context of both leaders and _____.
19. Politicians are held in _____ (low, high) public esteem.
20. Our ideal leaders are usually _____ (dead, alive).
21. We probably expect too (much, little) _____ of politicians.

Knowledge Objective: To define the various kinds of leadership
22. A leader without _____ is a contradiction in terms.
23. As political brokers, the coalition builders try to work out _____ between divergent groups.
24. _____ is the lifeblood of democracy.
25. Our political system depends on people willing to compete for _____.
26. Managers and leaders (do, do not) _____ require the same skills.
27. One reason why people run for office is to satisfy _____ needs.
28. There (is, is not) _____ a single effective style that all leaders should learn and practice.
29. One reason why people do not run for office is due to a loss of _____.

Knowledge Objective: To review the democratic faith
30. _____ is one of the best predictors of voting.
31. Thomas Jefferson believed there is nothing in the country that cannot be cured by good _____ and sound _____.
32. Our political system is far from perfect, but it is still an _____ system.

PART IV — POST-TEST

1. The principal objective of the framers was
   a. efficient government.
   b. representative government.
   c. individual liberty.
   d. responsive representatives.

2. The virtues of our present political system include
   a. easy leadership.
   b. safeguards against tyranny.
   c. decisive action.
   d. quick response to majorities.

3. The framers were *least* interested in making the government
   a. moderate.
   b. balanced.
   c. safe.
   d. efficient.

123

4. In the last days of Athenian democracy, the most common aspiration was for
   a. liberty.
   b. freedom.
   c. security.
   d. equality.

5. One of the greatest spokesmen for an educated citizenry was
   a. Alexander Hamilton.
   b. John Adams.
   c. Warren Harding.
   d. Thomas Jefferson.

6. The full operation of majority rule is slowed by all of the following *except*
   a. federalism.
   b. free elections.
   c. Bill of Rights.
   d. checks and balances.

7. People are reluctant to run for public office due to
   a. media criticism.
   b. campaign expenses.
   c. fear of compromising principles.
   d. all of the above.

8. In writing the Constitution, all of the following goals were sought *except*
   a. a government that would work.
   b. individual liberty.
   c. responsive government.
   d. preservation of strong local governments.

9. Crucial to the democratic faith is the belief that a constitutional democracy cherishes
   a. rule by force.
   b. majority rule.
   c. the free play of ideas.
   d. rule by the better and the wise.

10. People run for political office in order to
    a. advance fresh ideas.
    b. gain a voice in policy making.
    c. to gain prominence and power.
    d. all of the above

11. Unlike managers, leaders are primarily concerned with
    a. doing the right thing.
    b. doing things at the right time.
    c. doing things the right way.
    d. doing things.

12. Leaders are most concerned with
    a. doing the right thing.
    b. efficiency.
    c. the short term.
    d. none of the above

13. Which of the following is more likely to occur under a system of "broker rule"?
    a. unchecked majority rule
    b. clearly defined programs
    c. inability to compromise
    d. changing group pressures

14. Today, Americans tend to expect
    a. nothing from the government.
    b. reasonable actions from government.
    c. too little from government.
    d. too much from their government.

15. Who said "terrorist attacks can shake the foundations of our biggest buildings, but they cannot touch the foundation of America"?
    a. George W. Bush
    b. Colin Powell
    c. Dick Cheney
    d. Bill Clinton

PART V — TEST ANSWERS

Pretest

1. d	6. b	11. a
2. c	7. d	12. b
3. a	8. a	13. b
4. b	9. a	14. c
5. b	10. a	15. b

Programmed Review

1. will
2. faith; skepticism
3. authoritarian
4. obligation
5. security
6. active
7. terrorist
8. Liberty
9. grants; withholds
10. national; state
11. was not
12. against
13. majorities
14. balanced
15. broker
16. minority or opposition
17. are
18. followers
19. low
20. dead
21. much
22. power
23. compromises
24. Politics
25. office
26. do not
27. ego
28. is not
29. privacy
30. Education
31. newspapers; school masters
32. open

Post-test

1.	c	6.	b	11.	a
2.	b	7.	d	12.	c
3.	d	8.	d	13.	a
4.	c	9.	c	14.	b
5.	d	10.	d	15.	c